CEREMONIES
of the
LIVING SPIRIT

CEREMONIES
of the
LIVING SPIRIT

by

JOSEPH RAEL

(Beautiful Painted Arrow)

Council Oak Books
Tulsa / San Francisco

Council Oak Publishing Company, Inc.
Tulsa, OK 74120
©1998 by Joseph Rael. All rights reserved
First edition
00 99 98   8 7 5 4 3 2 1

Library of Congress Cataloging in Publication Data
Rael, Joseph.
      Ceremonies of the living spirit / Joseph E. Rael
      (Beautiful Painted Arrow).
         p.   cm.

      ISBN 1-57178-055-6 (pbk.   :   alk. paper)

      1. Shamanism—Miscellanea.   2. Rites and
      ceremonies—Miscellanea. 3. Tigua Indians—Rites
      and ceremonies—Miscellanea.   I. Title.
      BF1623.R6R43   1997
      299'.74—dc21   97-27077
                                                       CIP

Book and jacket design by Carl Brune

contents

appendix

We are the land dancing.

We live a life of prayer,

of reverence for the land,

a life of ceremony,

 so that we may stay alive

and connected to God.

God is present in the land:

the soil, the sky, the clouds,

the seasons, the climate.

And we are part of that design.

Chic a min ting . . .

*i*n the Tiwa language of the Picuris Pueblo, storytellers begin with *"chic a min ting"*— a long time ago. Literally, *chic a min ting* means "at the sand place." We use this expression to mean "a long time ago" because every grain of sand is an eternity and there are many of them.

What does sand come from? From *naa meh nay*. Soil. Sand is the soil along the ocean—the ocean, which is a portrayal of the cosmic mind.

Puns, metaphors, parables, and stories are the teaching tools of the spiritual teacher in every tradition, including mine. Metaphors connect the world around us with the metaphysical, giving us a window on the infinite.

A metaphor is not simply a figure of speech. Metaphor is how God is present in our lives. We think in godly ways because metaphor is energy that is in a state of action, breathing life into ceremony. We work with metaphor in order to find the essence of everything we encounter in the material world, in perceptual reality. We trace it back through metaphor, and when we trace it back, we find that everything is connected to the heavens. When we trace the language, it all ties back to the One.

Everything that exists is trying to unify itself with that whole. All ceremony exists to unify, to bring together, to bring into oneness — but within that oneness is the diversity of all that is.

The oneness is, actually, the only thing that exists. It is the only reality. And it is nothing. Yet from that nothing comes all that is.

The land is who we are. The land is our first significant energy, which we begin to recognize as ourselves. The land is where our power really lies, and that is where supernatural power can be cultivated.

There is a supernatural power that every human being has, that cannot be cultivated by reading and writing. We must do something with our physical bodies and natural elements of the land, the fire, water, air, minerals, and wood. Native American ceremonies, some of which are very ancient, and many of the secret societies that Indians have, are based on this intention: to reconnect, over and over and over, to the land. When we keep connected with the land, that's how we can keep our power.

We find life empty and unsatisfying or uninspiring because we don't do enough ceremony. It is encoded in our physical make-up, by virtue of the fact that we have eyes and ears and mouths and noses and legs, that we are here to be catalysts and to connect the physical with the spiritual. And ceremony is how we do that.

Actually, in a sense, everything we do is ceremony, whether we mean it that way or not. But ceremony is so much more powerful if we do it intentionally. Ceremonies we do intentionally as ceremony focus our energies on certain acts and lift us powerfully into states of consciousness through which we are literally drinking light. We are drinking inspiration from all the heavens and connecting the above realms with the physical plane. This is what we come into physical form to do, and we are nurtured by doing it. If we don't have enough ceremony in our lives, pretty soon we feel empty and sad and dispirited.

We may think we're sad because our physical needs aren't met or we need more success, but what we're really feeling is the natural hunger of the self for connection with the vast Self. And that can only come through ceremony.

Ceremonies are most powerful if we do them regularly as a part of a community of people who gather for that purpose. They can be done alone; in fact, we came into this physical form to express an individual, particular vibration or essence. But really, we are connected with each other and with the vast Self, and we need to reconnect regularly, because that is the source of our joy, the source of our energy, the source of our enthusiasm or zest for life.

The ceremonies have to do with chanting. Chanting has to do with sound. Sound has to do

with the vibration of the spirit that is in the land.
In ceremony, we are the land chanting, we are the
land dancing.

There is a voice that now is coming from the
land. It wants to tell its story, and this is its time.
It is time for the land to tell its story.

voice of silence

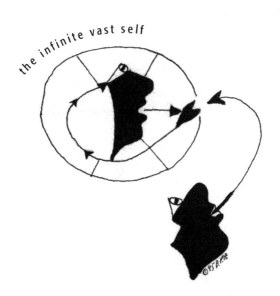

the infinite vast self

entering the metaphoric mind

*W*hen I was about eight, I had three languages that I was learning simultaneously: Spanish, English, and Tiwa. Up until that time I had only spoken Ute. Learning these three languages at the same time made me aware of the difference of languages, and the similarities. I began to understand the symbolic power of language.

In order to learn the languages, I had to listen very carefully to the sounds. Like a child learning to read, I "sounded out" words. I came to the realization that sounds, especially vowel sounds, are the vibrations of principal ideas, encoded in the human gene pool, and words made from these sounds will carry within them the principal ideas that are the same, no matter what language a person is speaking.

Eventually, I developed an understanding of the principal ideas behind each of the five vowel sounds:

A = purification

E = placement

I = awareness

O = childlike innocence

U = carrying

Using this knowledge, I can go beyond the surface meaning of a word in Tiwa or Spanish or English or whatever language, to discover the principal ideas with which it is connected. I can chant the vowel sounds in a word like "table" or "walking" and connect on a vibrational level with the principal ideas which created those forms.

The other thing I learned, or at least what I was taught, was that when in Rome, it was important to do as the Romans do. The Ute language was appropriate for the geography of the Ute reservation in southern Colorado. When my mother died and I was taken to live with my father's people in Northern New Mexico, I was taught Tiwa, because it was the power of language for that place — for the Picuris Pueblo. The Tiwa language is like an energy that resonates in that geography. I was eating from that resonance, sleeping it, so I needed to speak it. Tiwa was the vibration of that geography, which extended for twenty or thirty miles.

Everything that exists on the surface of the land is really an extension of the land. Ceremonies are about these extensions of land, or how land expresses itself in its highest natural form.

And land is the symbol of the vast Self that is in a state of purification. Land is flowing with waters that purify, with rivers, with rain, with snow, with the ocean like a big lung, constantly freshening the air.

In Tiwa, land is *naa meh nay*. The first sound is *Nah*. *Nah* means Self, the Self in a state of purification. *Meh* means movement. How is a state of movement occurring on the land? How is the land producing movement? How is the land producing placement and connection? How is land connecting the sky and the earth? Life is unfolding from the inner recesses of land, which is really the Self, the vast Self.

The land is telling the story. It is not a story about Tiwa people; it is not a story about any tribe. This is the story of the land, the vast Self, speaking about what it knows it is.

That is what consciousness is. Consciousness is the result of how the vast Self is in a state of movement, how it is purifying itself, how it is placing itself, how it is manifesting.

For instance, we've developed a technology around materialism, and after many years of developing the technology, we have come to think that this is a material universe. Yet there is another universe that exists alongside it, and it is called breath. We haven't really dealt with that universe. We haven't understood that metaphor. We have separated ourselves; we've said, "This is scientific; that isn't." What we need to do now is understand how the soul purifies itself so that it connects concreteness with abstractness— concreteness, which is the material, with spirituality, inspiration. This book is about how inspiration occurs and how in the process it purifies that form of placement that we can now experience between ourselves as material beings and a philosophy or abstractness, or breath, or inspiration. We can now use our inspirations to materialize our goals and objectives that are not in detriment to our highest spirit.

When traditional Native American people look at material reality, we are looking not for scientific truth, but for the metaphors. To look at a thing as metaphor is to ask, "What principal idea is it expressing?"

We are born into the realm of discovery. This is the gift that allows us to enter into the world of sound which is encoded in our gene pool. Another way of saying this is we innately know how to speak in metaphor because the void is the timelessness of what we know as the "here and now." The void is essentially the No-mind. Consequently, as soon as the thinking mind enters into the void of the No-mind, the action of that motion awakens the remembering of the gene pool. It is at this point that we know what we did not *think* we knew.

Everything is metaphor. Everything that exists — every object, every action, every experience — is expressing some principal idea. Therefore, it is important for us, early in life, to pursue ways of conceptualization that enhance metaphor alongside experience. Ceremonies of the living spirit are such pathways. They give us routes to follow so we can penetrate the surface of manifested reality and experience directly the power of principal ideas.

For instance, suppose we want to understand the meaning of the Council Oak tree. The Western mind would see the tree from a practical standpoint, as a place where people could have shade, as a central gathering place. In the Tiwa language of my people, treeness means "opening," and opening means abundance in childlike innocence In Tiwa, the tree is *daul ool*, and *daul* means abundance, and *ooo* means innocence and teachability. So therefore, when you came under the Council Oak tree, you would come because there you would automatically be innocent and teachable.

The Indians came in to gather around the Council Oak tree because the oak is the symbol of life. They came to talk about life issues around the tree which is the essence of teachability. So when the Indians came together to talk at the

Council Oak, they knew, either consciously or unconsciously, that, since technically we do not exist and since we are basically our own perceptions, if we then perceive ourselves as teachable, or if we perceive ourselves as states of abundance, that idea would dominate the gathering. That idea is like the keynote speaker. The keynote determines what is going to be spoken in that conference. The Council Oak tree would be a place where you could break all the old rules and start fresh.

Everything is encoded in the gene pool. Whatever language we speak, we are speaking from that particular culture, but beneath that there is a code that is understood universally. One of the ways to tap into this code is to listen to how we pronounce words. Sounds are important. For instance, the sound "waa" in English is part of the word "one." *Waa* in Tiwa means life. Behind both of these is a common essential idea which is encoded in the human gene pool.

In order to become conscious of all of that, we have ceremony. When we dance a bear dance on the reservation or we dance a corn dance, it is our way of expressing devotion for the Holiest of All Holies. For me, dancing is like going to church. My whole body is in prayer when I am dancing. Sometimes I dance my anxieties, to pray about them by dancing them. When something comes up for me or I need answers, I just go dance. Dancing, in metaphor, means to expand. We dance to expand our awareness.

When we dance in ceremony, we are expanding whatever principle that we are dancing at that time. For instance, if we are doing the circle dance, we are casting new seeds of understanding, since the seed and the circle are metaphors of the same principal idea. Yet we are not consciously aware of that in that moment, as we dance.

The planet made it possible for us to be here. The planet, the spiritual essence of the vast Self which is made up of valleys and rivers and mountains and oceans, is really the concrete formulation of infinite nothingness. Infinite nothingness has now become concreteness, in the form of oceans, valleys, rivers, water, oxygen...

We need to look at the fact that in our consciousness we have somehow separated ourselves from ourselves and from God. Perhaps we wanted to be better than God. In doing so, we have created disease, because, being separate from God, we have been functioning only at half power.

When we are born we leave the wholeness of the mother. We break off, become individualized. We say, "I'm going to read and write. I'm going to be a master of my own life. I'm going to run my life the way I want to. I'm going to be on my own." That's fine, and we have developed a technology that allows that, but we have separated ourselves more from ourselves, from the infinite Self, from the vast Self, from the God Self.

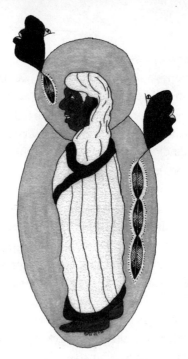

Mother Earth, Father Sky

Yet we are really part of *naa-meh-nay*. If you want to know what is wrong with you, you go back to what is wrong in the land. The Indians say, "Don't cut up Mother Earth." With all our technology, we lose touch with the land, with *nah-meh-nay*, and when we lose touch with the land, we lose touch with ourselves and with the vast Self.

The word *naa-meh-nay* tells us that the Self is in a state of movement, and movement is manifestation. *Naa* is the Self. *Meh* is movement. *Naa meh nay*, then, means that the earth is the Self in a state of movement. The word speaks of closeness to higher planes of knowledge, of knowing. It speaks of sky energy, of what is up above, in touch with high spiritual beings of all ages.

Land is the principal form that sets up a step ladder to climb to the heavens, because the land is the vast Self, which is descending light that purifies; it is the purifying force that brings heaven and earth together and crystallizes it so that it looks like a tree or an elephant or an ocean. Any time you have movement there is manifestation, and manifestation brings perception. When I touch or feel or see something with my physical senses, that is perception.

Matter is in a state of incompleteness; it must have the perception of the perceiver to exist. Matter is temporary. It only keeps its form for as long as we think it is what we think it is, and then we change it to something else. Its meaning is temporary.

When something is no longer applicable, it ceases to take form. We're not making many lances anymore, or arrows, because they are not applicable. They are obsolete; they don't matter anymore. We don't have many horses anymore because we go out there and get in our Cadillacs. That's our new metaphor for the horse.

You see, we don't really need to drive cars. Easily and quickly, within a few hours if we had to, we could come up with other means of transportation—means that don't rely on material things like cars. But we've chosen to drive cars because we're trying to get to Beauty materialistically.

We're not going to get there that way, of course. The way to God is through inspiration. But because we are connected to the economics of our time, we move according to how much money we can make, and so we're trapped by our own desire for economic security, and we miss out on creating nonmaterial modes of transportation. There are many inventions that haven't appeared because they're not proper to the social, political, and economic systems we've created. They're not in line with what we consider to be self-preservation.

The true inspirations will not come until there is true poverty. As long as we continue to have plenty of cars and airplanes, we'll continue to have that form of transportation. But suppose there is a scarcity of aluminum and steel and rubber tires. I would guess that within twenty-four hours we would have an invention. Within a month, we would have a whole other kind of system going for transportation.

In order to understand why we're doing what we're doing today, we have to understand the goals and objectives of people one hundred fifty years ago. And, as we change our ideas about reality, we change reality for people who come after us. That is because, when we change our ideas about reality, we change our actions. We go to a different orientation.

When I am in Albuquerque, I think to myself, someone a long time ago looked up toward Santa Fe and said, "I am going to have to be there in three days and I wish I had more time with those people up in Santa Fe, but I'm going to have to walk maybe a day and half to get there, and I wish there was a faster way." Well, maybe somebody thought that a hundred years ago and now we have cars that take us from Albuquerque to Santa Fe in an hour. Somebody thought of it and then later materialized it and now we have pavement and we have cars and we complain because there is pollution in Albuquerque and Santa Fe. But somebody dreamed it up back then. So, I guess the moral of the story is be careful what you dream about, because you'll probably get it.

Sometimes I can see thoughts manifesting as if they were lights. I see thoughts travel across a room in little blocks of light about half an inch long and a quarter of an inch wide. There are spaces in between when one of those little blocks of light ends and before the next one begins. These spaces are when that thought is open and is ready to manifest new form, even as it's going along. That's how quickly change can occur. Even as we are thinking something out, as it is traveling twenty feet across a room, it can change.

Life is a circle and the circle means seed. Any time we have a thought, we have just seeded an idea into the vastness, which is made of the land, which is made of earth and sky. The breath is *haah*. *Haah* is identity; breath is identity. Breath gives identity to movement; it gives identity to relationships and to the hierarchy of knowledge as we seek to understand the mystery. Breath connects us with higher levels. Breath is inspiration. Breath inspires things to occur, because the breath is an integral part of how the miraculous is unfolding on the material level, in the material plane. Without breath, nothing occurs.

We think breath is just physical, but the reason we are breathing all the time is that this is how we stay spiritual. Breathing is how landscape stays spiritual. The land breathes and it rains and the wind blows. Maybe it brings tornadoes or hurricanes, but the breath is still spiritual. One inspiration comes and soon another one comes, and soon after another comes. In this reality, this land of *wah mah chi* (breath, matter, and movement), there has to be a continual, perpetual state of inspiration because everything is impermanent. In this plane of reality, there is always a continuum of becoming something we want to become without ever really becoming what we want to become, because that which exists as a state of impermanence does not really exist.

This material plane is where we go to find out how to get where we want to go, only to learn we've already arrived. But we are still trying to get there. The exciting part is that we are still talking about process. That is what the earth is about: process. When we understand what process is, then we know why we need to be here.

By participating in the process of a ceremony, we can reconnect ourselves with the vast Self. And so we dance a Circle Dance, and we become the power of completion or oneness.

Or we cover ourselves with clay in a ceremony, and by doing so we remake ourselves back into land. By doing that we reconnect our psyche back from splitness to wholeness. When we connect to vast Self, whatever we create after that is going to be inspired by things that are in tune with the highest potential of the planet as a whole.

We call the claying ceremony an Initiation into Womanhood. We dig a hole and then someone stands there, and a woman who is an elder, at least fifty-five years old, puts mud on the person standing in the hole. As she is doing this, the rest of us stand outside the hole and we sing sounds. When the vibration of our voices comes on the skin of the initiate and on the water, she is initiated into womanhood. We do the same thing for the men. The men initiate themselves into womanhood so they can unfold in the feminine. We do this so we can now bring the feminine and the masculine together. Womanhood allows the seed within life to germinate into the soil of life, the soil of landscape.

We all want to be initiated into womanhood because it is the feminine that helps us to slip through the crack between the two slices of light, and for a split of a split second, we exist. It's the feminine, not the masculine, that is that power of inspiration. When the inspiration unfolds, then it is masculine. The feminine is the descending light itself, and the masculine is the unfolding of the feminine.

In ceremony we are rededicating ourselves to the original goal of the vast Self, which is the land. The land may look like Scotland, or Italy, or Germany, or South America or the United States. But it is really just the Self—the vast Self—and the noosphere.

Noosphere is a word coined by Teilhard de Chardin which means a light-like band of energy, full of the power of lifting, that encircles material reality as the atmosphere encircles the earth. When I use the term, I mean that part of the vast Self that is lifted, or that is lifting. The noosphere is a symbol of the Self that is lifting so anything that comes from there is going to kick you upstairs. The noosphere is a force that is lifting the vast Self.

Another way of explaining the noosphere might be to compare it to a halo or aura around the human head.

The head is the planet Earth and the halo or aura of the person is the noosphere.

Inside the human brain is the thalamus—the relay or association center which integrates

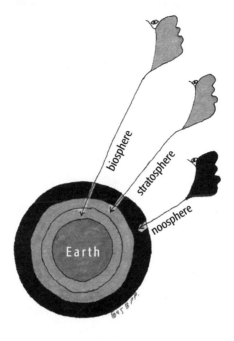

emotions with experience. The thalamus connects the heart with the head. The thalamus is at the "heart" or center of the brain, and it lies beneath the cerebrum—the seat of rationality—which is at the periphery of the brain. In Tiwa thought, the center, or heart, is connected with hot, with summer, and with emotions, while the periphery is the place of the cold, rational winter energy. In the pueblo, we have summer people and winter people whose activities in this earth plane balance the hot with the cold through ceremonies.

Ceremony is to awaken the child's memory. It's done once a year so that we reinstill a pattern in everybody; we reawaken that ancient process by which the heart and the mind create balance in the living Earth.

The Earth is made of spirit (winds, thunder, lightening), mind (land), and body (movement within matter). The Earth is made of *wah mah chi*:

> *Wah* means spirit;
> *Mah* means mind;
> *Chi* means body.

Speaking in very general terms only, an idea is given birth into linear time following these steps:

First, the spirit (*wah*) breathes, inspires the idea to become;

Secondly, the mind (*mah*) brings it into a place of manifested consciousness. Now the new idea has a mind.

Finally, the *chi* is the movement of the new idea in the physical body. Hence, life is breath, matter, and movement. The nature of the movement of the earth spinning around the sun is the force which pulls into the earth the idea from Spirit (sky) and captures it in the land (*mah*) and gives it movement (*chi*) (eyes to see as in perceptual reality). An idea (or ideal) is born.

The long dances, drum dances, and sun dances awaken ideas toward expanding holistically, because during the dancing the body heats up and cools off, thereby integrating the mental and emotional bodies.

Tiwa people believe that two-leggeds— humans—came to this earth to bring reconciliation. Our job is to be the catalysts for the reconciliation of ideas. It is a part of the process that began when the unity of the vast Self began to perceive itself as diversity. Out of that diversity came polarity. We are here to act on that polarity to help bring about reconciliation.

We are the catalysts for this reconciliation because we have two legs. In the process of walking, we balance and reconcile polarities of left and right.

The word for "walk" in Tiwa is *tah chi who*:

Tah   means to plow, or to seed;

Chi   means movement, especially a movement of reconciliation;

Who   means carrying, or right action.

Inherent in the word *tah chi who* is the understanding that by walking we are implanting this earth plane with the sort of movement that will carry, or bring balance—that will reconcile polarities.

As we walk our destiny as two-leggeds, we will find ourselves designing new technologies that are in balance with our ecosystem. This is the purpose of our specific task as humans. We walk so that we can transform ourselves—genetically and in other ways—to continue our evolution.

Henceforth, new technologies created by mankind will be more in tune with the needs of the earth and sky.

The wind comes to bring to the earth

Two parts of carrying power, one part of awareness, one part of Self, one part of movement.

It is what provides us with the Breath of Life.

The thinking and the No-mind bring us the transcendence made of how to crystallize our completions, of how to find awareness in our lives.

They teach us how to keep on plowing awareness into our Beauty that is filled with Good Works. And too, That Which Comes

Celebrates when we find ourselves in the actions of the Infinite Right Action.

In the weather pattern of the earth we have lows and highs (pressure systems) that determine our weather. Every once in a while we experience inversions. In Tiwa thought, this pushing and pulling, heating and cooling of air, this work, is the same thing as worship. ("Work is worship," my grandfather told me.) In other words, these highs and lows and inversions are how the electromagnetism pulls in or pushes ideas from the *core* of the earth to the biosphere, stratosphere, and noosphere; or from the noosphere to the stratosphere to the biosphere. These understandings of how new ideas take form in material reality are Tiwa teachings. Of course, the Tiwa elders did not use scientific words like noosphere and stratosphere and biosphere. They taught in metaphors, and in the Tiwa language, which is itself rich in metaphor.

On the other hand, the initiation into womanhood I described earlier is not done in the way I described as a Tiwa tradition or a Southern Ute tradition. I am here to create tradition. Everything that I do, I do from my visions. I am a visionary.

All ceremony originally came from a vision somebody had which gave instructions for exercising mystical power. The instructions were passed down from generation to generation unchanged, because if they were changed they would lose their power. The Tiwa creation stories were told over and over, from year to year, using exactly the same words. They still are. They are only to be told in the winter. They aren't just children's stories; they are really a source of mystical power. The storytellers repeat the stories not just because the new children coming up need to hear them. The very pronunciation of the words of the story is affecting the psyche of the planetary resonance. It is affecting not only the Tiwa world but all of the world — from New York to France to the Polar regions. That's why it is very important to tell them in the same way every time.

It's the same with any traditional ceremony that belongs to a people or a tribe. It has to be done in the same way each time to work, whether it's a ceremony for healing or for bringing rain or for whatever purpose. These stories are sacred and their telling is a ceremony. They were never to be written down in their exact form, and one man who told them to anthropologists to be written down was banished from Picuris for life. When I was studying art in Santa Fe Indian School there was a lot of discussion among the Puebloans that we shouldn't be selling pottery or weavings or paintings if they had the Pueblo's sacred symbols on them because a person can't sell sacred things.

For these reasons, I don't teach Picuris (Tiwa) religion or Ute religion. I teach what has come to me from my visions. I spent fifty years becoming a visionary, so that what I do in ceremony comes from Source and it works. I don't know how these ceremonies work or why they work, but they work. People who criticize me for sharing ceremonies with non-Indians don't understand that the ceremonies I am doing are not traditional or tribal.

I believe that this is a way of bringing people who really want to know the Spirit into the context of the Spirit, so that they will know their own inner source and how to bring that forth in their lives in an active way and awaken their own spiritual awareness. Maybe that's our job, to make that connection with books or art or ceremonies. Maybe we help that awakening to manifest in a quicker way for individuals who want to pursue the mystical resonances of their own inner sources into blossoming forms. To me, that's why we write books and do art and music.

Now if there were five hundred people and I said to them that I am a visionary and everything that I do comes from my vision, 467 of them might say, "We are not going to be involved with it because you are not coming out of scripture, and therefore we are not going to believe that." If they want to say that, that's fine. Remember, we live in *perceptual* reality. Perceptual reality has five aspects, and one of those five is purity. Purists say, "If it's not real, then I don't want it." Yet I believe we are all visionaries and that we come out of inspiration. After all, we have been breathing since we were born, haven't we?

We get an idea, we get inspired and decide that this is how we have to do it now. We say, "*Ah-ha!*"

"*Ah-ha*" is the word for inspiration; it is also the word for breath.

When we initiate women or men, we are initiating them for the planet and for the cosmos. Apparently this initiation is needed right now or we wouldn't be talking about it. The ideas that we are getting come from the noosphere. The planet knows what it needs.

Often we don't understand the message and we go off in left field. I believe this is because we still think we are better than God. We have to get back to our integration with the land, and then our thoughts are going to be in tune with environmental consciousness. All we need is a handful of people to be initiated. Perhaps we could initiate seven thousand women and seven thousand men over a period of time, and that would restabilize the planet. Our initiation restabilizes the unfolding of the feminine for everyone.

That is my job. That is what I chose to do when I finally ended up with two feet and here in this lifetime. Consciousness was just unfolding in life's greatness and having a great ball of fun. Soon enough, I was more than a twinkle in my father's eye and I came and I was born. Now here I am, and I am part of an ancient people who believe that the land is the inifinte Self and that what it means to be a human being is to have vision. We honor the visionaries in our world as seers because of what they know. They have given their lives to do what they do, and they are the only ones who have accessed this information until some time when everybody will have access to it.

A visionary knows the meaning behind very ordinary things. For instance, what does it mean when you are walking down some stairs and there's a low ceiling and you accidentally hit your head? In metaphor, it means that the universe is asking you to focus on something. You notice that when you hit yourself.

Maybe you feel stupid. I think what the psyche is saying is that there is separation between thought and body. Thought and body need to be put together again. To me the body (including its feelings) represents the land, the vast Self. The thoughts and the brain are what comes out of the vast Self, but the brain sees itself as separate from the vast Self because it kind of sits up there on its throne and wants to run things, control things. That is fine for a while, but eventually it has to understand that it is not independent and it has to merge and come together in the vastness of the vast Self in order to touch reality.

Technological society encourages the separation of the mind from the body. Our educational system, and everything that we really value in Western culture, separates us from our infinite Self.

I have heard certain speakers say that clergy took our spirituality and doctors took our physical bodies and the universities took our minds, so we are a separated, fragmented society. We rely on specialization, whereas in the beginning everything was all under one being, one thing together. We are fragmented in the house of shattering light—which is consciousness. What we want to do is get back together again.

Unification has to be done almost all the time, and that is why we have rituals and ceremonies we repeat. Every several days we do a ceremony to renew our unification again. This is the power of the ceremonial cycle. The effect of each individual ritual accumulates over time as it is repeated. By having a monthly ceremony or a weekly ceremony, we reinforce our connection to the whole, like the nerve connected to the whole brain.

The Catholic mass is a good example. In Catholicism as I see it, as soon as you go into that setting, into that church, you go back into the infinite Self, back into the soul, back into the center, back into that part of you that you separated from. It is like returning to the womb. There are symbols that the genetic pool knows and the unconscious responds to. A candle is the light, the truth. The priest is the metaphor for the inner self, that is, for the soul.

The drink is the sweetness of life, the wine, the sweet blood of life. It is in the cardiovascular system on the physical level, but we are not talking about physical so much as we are talking about the spiritual cardiovascular system, the mental cardiovascular system, and the emotional cardiovascular system.

The bread is beautiful light. When two or more come together and break the bread they are eating beautiful light. As they do this, they remember, on some level, that they are the light of beauty.

The being of emotion is breathing, it is thinking. It is perception. Perception has to do with knowing—knowing through the senses and also knowing beyond the senses.

I think someone has already said these things. What we are doing is making it so ordinary and natural that people are really going to understand it. Because it *is* natural, and it is all around us, and it is made of land and movement and breathing.

Land is *naa-meh-nay*, which is the Self fusing itself with matter in a way that has a relationship to everything else that is happening at that moment in time, and connecting to all the heavenly planes. *Naa-meh-nay* exists so that the Self can connect to physical materialism and to the spiritual aspect of Earth.

In Tiwa the word *naa-meh-nay* is what the land is doing, what land is being. When we say *naa-meh-nay* it is not a fixed thing. *Naa* is Self, *meh* is movement. *Naa-meh-nay* is the Self that purifies, that connects the material to the spiritual through movement.

To the degree that we lift ourselves to a higher level of being is the degree that we have physical movement on the planet. And we keep lifting. When we have earthquakes and disasters, we suffer loss. Perhaps people die. Yet, we can look at it both ways: we can ask what is the lesson? What is the blessing? If I am a materialist, I will say, "No! It is not good, because I just lost five parking lots in that earthquake. That was my income." Maybe the gift for me in losing five parking lots is that now I am going to have to figure a different way to make a living. And in the process of figuring that out, I am going to change my psyche and that is going to give me *naa-meh-nay*, the Self in the state of movement, manifesting something new.

Naa-meh-nay is telling its story. If we will listen carefully, perhaps we might reconnect ourselves for an instant to the heavenly planes. Perhaps we might, for a split of a split second, really exist.

Wah mah chi

*i*n the beginning, according to the creation story, there was nothing. All was complete blankness. This nothingness wanted to bring itself into awareness, to know itself.

Then, life was created by *Wah-mah-chi*, which is the Tiwa name for God, and means breath, matter, and movement. The breath is the inspiration in matter that brings all concreteness, or form, into existence via movement. Really only one thing exists, and that is the breath of God in a state of movement creating the vibration of matter.

When the Supreme Being breathed into the space of nothing, this created intent. This intent was divine calling — divine longing — creating matter in movement toward a particular direction. The word for "intent" in Tiwa is *poh-cheh*. *Poh* is "blowing breath" and *cheh* means eyes. *Poh-cheh*, then, literally means "Blowing breath with eyes that see." With intent, or *poh-cheh*, perceptual reality was created.

In this creation time, the Great Mystery breathed into this nothingness and created the intent, the blowing breath with eyes that see, or perceptual reality. The intent was an integral part of heart. There was then the heart center—what we would later know as truth. And this heart center was connected to purity, and this purity was connected to beauty, and this beauty would bond all things.

As breath came into this space of nothingness, there was a mist like a white cloud, created by the tears of joy of the breath. The blowing breath, with eyes to see how it was creating, was now streaming with tears — rivers of consciousness. This water then began to fall onto the earth. The Tiwa storyteller tells us that this first rainfall was the light coming from God. As it descended, it went down through endless space until it reached and touched the first essence of matter. Then matter and spirit began to create all of the eternities, and one of those eternities would be ours.

At that beginning, the land and the people and the sky were different manifestations of metaphor alongside experience. For every experience that was occurring, there was a metaphor to substantiate it.

This is how sound and imagery create physical form — matter. Without imagery and sound — sound which is made of vibration — matter cannot be created.

Sound is the first phenomenon. In Tiwa, *poh* means "blowing breath," and it also means sound—vibration that is in a state of being heard or experienced as audible. *Poh* also means the circle of the medicine wheel. Thus, sound and the medicine wheel are synonymous.

Imagery came after sound. First was *poh*, then came imagery to fill in the *poh*, the first circle of light. Imagery is the combination of a number of essences that came together from the vast infinite Self in the very earliest moments of creation to form the stream of consciousness inside of the circle of life, or medicine wheel. Those essences included awareness, manifestation, purity, goodness, relativity, radiance, and the capacity of transcendence. (Relativity is placement, and it is our connectedness with all things. Radiance is that essence that gives us our highs and lows.)

Without imagery, matter could not be created. To make matter required movement of awareness in the play of a number of essences such as purity, goodness, relativity, radiance, and transcendence, or combinations of these. *I-ma-ge-ry*. The sound that it makes tells what it means: "To create while keeping a close watch over what is created, once it is given birth, so that life may know itself."

I now see this creation as a continual process, an evolution of consciousness that results from an interplay between the noosphere, or the realm of pure ideas, and the material realm. It is like a continual exchange of breath. Life energy (*waaa*), or inspiration, descends into the medicine wheel from the noosphere.

An image of creation comes to me from the important ceremonies of my two peoples. My Tiwa people hold a festival day each August 10 at

Picuris Pueblo, which climaxes with the climbing of a pole. Before the day begins, a pole about twenty-five feet tall has been cut from a tree on the mountain, brought down, and set up in the center of the pueblo. This pole becomes the heart-center of the village. At the top of this pole are tied a sheep, a basket of bread, and a watermelon. After a day of sacred ceremonies, feasting, running, and dancing, clown dancers emerge from the kiva and try to climb the pole. Climbing the pole is not easy, and only the strongest men can do it. But eventually, one of the clowns or another young man from the pueblo succeeds in getting to the top. When he does, he unties the sheep, the bread, and the watermelon, and brings them down to the people in the village.

Among my Southern Ute people, an annual sun dance is held during which people who are fasting from food and water dance back and forth to the sun dance pole (made from a tree which was cut down and placed in the middle of the sun dance circle). The sun dance circle is circumscribed by trees and represents the medicine wheel.

When I saw the clowns climbing up and down the pole at Picuris, and when I took part in the Ute sun dance, I understood creation as a flash of new inspiration that was being brought to the Earth from a higher plane. In the Tiwa language, the word for "people" also means "vibration." The people feed on this new inspiration (the vibration is changed), and consciousness is pushed upward, symbolized both at Picuris and the Southern Ute Sun dance by the fact that a new pole replaces the old one each year.

The pole climb or the sun dance pole was the Indians' way to recreate how perceptual reality comes into being. These ceremonies re-enact how life is perpetually in a state of creativity.

Of course, there is no "up-and-down" continuum in reality. We create these metaphors here in order to give purity, placement, awareness, innocence and carrying a structure. Only when these are ordered in a linear structure, oriented in time, can we perceive that which cannot be seen outside space and time.

The medicine wheel is the basic structure, or the essential metaphor, for all that is. Picture a medicine wheel, a circle divided into four parts. Think of the segments as winter in the north quadrant, spring in the east, summer in the south and autumn in the west. There is a line between winter and spring, showing the equinox where winter ends and spring begins. It is my understanding that exactly at that line is an opening which allows, and in fact demands, for new ideas to enter. Right at the line between winter and spring, new ideas enter via a slice of light into the medicine wheel. These lines between the seasons represent gates or doorways. Among my people, it is believed that there are gatekeepers. These gatekeepers are referred to as grandmothers or grandfathers, or in Tiwa as mother-father beings. Their responsibility is to let in the new ideas or to refuse their entry. At this precise point immediately after entry, *Chaa-ched* happens. *Chaa* means the here-and-now. *Cha* creates presentness in linear time. In the word *cha-ched,* the *ched* means that which is perceptive. Before *ched* we do not have cognition because we cannot perceive. *Ched* is the vibration of perception.

Cha creates a place for an idea to appear and be rooted — to display its wares — while *ched* assigns the perceptual dimension of that which is coming into being.

In the village of Picuris where I grew up, there is a stone we call "the Blue Stone people," which is a sacred site. Many times during my childhood I saw the elders of Picuris coming to the stone to honor the Blue Stone people and give them corn meal.

In 1987, while doing ceremonies in Pennsylvania, I had a vision which revealed to me the meaning behind the Blue Stone people, and, more than that, has brought me insight into the nature of creation, and how ideas take material form. In *Being and Vibration,* which I wrote in 1993 with Mary Elizabeth Marlow, I told about my vision:

> *It was as though I was standing behind a curtain which was clear but not transparent. Suddenly, the veil was pierced and a hole*

began to grow larger and larger until there was an opening into another dimension. There before me appeared a vast horizon.

In the vision I saw Picuris Pueblo, New Mexico, as it was thousands of years ago. It was at a time when the ocean water, which had previously covered it, was gone. All that remained was a mud flat.

I saw two beings descending from outer space. They were sitting side by side, riding on some kind of transparent space machine, the dimensions of which could be sensed rather than seen. They came closer and closer toward a place near where my grandmother's house was later to be built. Eventually, they landed.

As soon as they landed, I knew who they were: two kachina figures who had come to bring the spirit of life to the village. They were giant figures, at least ten feet tall, androgynous in nature, wearing long flowing black robes which contrasted sharply with the whitewash painted on their square-like faces. They landed at a place I could see had been previously designated as the sacred site for the new inhabitants who were to become the people high up in the mountains of north central New Mexico. And then, without warning, they were transformed into he/she Blue Stone people.

In another moment, I saw overlays of rapidly changing landscapes until suddenly my *grandmother's house appeared, as if coming out of the dawn-time of an early morning light and fresh air. There is a blue stone that sits outside my grandmother's house today. It is the same blue stone into which the kachinas were transformed. At the time of that transformation, the stone was anchored into the earth and there it remains, a major power point whose effect has been experienced for generations and will be experienced for generations to come.*

The vision then changed rapidly. I was moved through a time continuum. A dozen or so scenes were flashed before me. I saw the formation of the rivers and the mountains, the heating up and cooling down of the earth, lush, green vegetation and brown, arid dryness. Each era, each landscape, was a new page flashed before my eyes and then blown away by vigorous wind. As each page was removed, another appeared. The scenes lasted for only seconds but contained an eternity. Finally, the shifts ceased, and one scene remained. The scene looked like Picuris as it was in 1940 when I first saw it with my child's eyes.

It is interesting that the Tiwa creation stories have the beings from outer space who came here to seed the planet. That is part of the whole concept of consciousness, the concept of the upper world seeding the middle and lower worlds (the lower world being the land, the earth). These beings seed the earth with ideas—vibrations that enhance *naa-meh-nay*.

Out of that seeding emerges everything we know, according to the vision I had. The kachinas plant the seeds of what we know now as the circle of life or the sacred circle, or the medicine wheel. They bring time and timelessness. Nothing becomes something. What happens is that they seed the earth, which is the vastness of the vast Self. They come from up above; they come down on a transparent ship; and then they go back into the heavens and translate what this all means psychologically; and then they come back and land, not really landing on land. They stop, and things take material form. Infinite vastness is the beginning. That is what they land on. According to the vision that I saw, this is how spirit descends into matter.

Another way to say this is that in a split of a split second, a flash, a principal idea descends from the noosphere, into the infinite vastness. The noosphere is full of lifting ideas, so any time inspiration comes, it is because a thought has gone up and imprinted itself on the noosphere.

From the noosphere comes a downward flow of energy, undifferentiated energy, feminine energy, spirit. Infinite vastness stops the downward flow of this spirit energy. Spirit falls until the infinite Self stops it. It is still perceptual, not material. It is impermanence. Then it lands on the floor of life—the infinite Self.

The spirit is different from the infinite Self. It is transparent. It is like nothingness coming down, and it merges with the infinite Self and becomes something.

Another way to say this is to consider the Tiwa word *wa*. *Wa* is light descending—*wa,* as in the English word, *one*. One is everything coming together; one is up above and down below, north, south, east, and west. *Wa* is the light that precedes creation.

It meets the infinite Self and it is then two. Two means *to cry*; two means we can say, *"Hello there!"* or we can call out, or cry in tears, because we are now in reflection, in duality. We can now mirror, and we are the image.

The vast oneness has to split into the vast or infinite Self and spirit before anything can happen. As in the process of biology, the cells separate to make more cells and make life.

After separation, spirit and the infinite Self come together in a different way. The way in which they come together depends upon inspiration, which is the breath, or the imprint of the movement of *ni*. Inspiration, breath, or *ni* is materialization in which placement or relativity is an enactment of motion, and which instills wisdom in the act of making this placement in this moment.

In a later dream I saw more of how the creation took place. At first, after the waters started to recede, the land was there and it was just a lot of rocks. Then the winter came; I could see the snow, and then I could see it melting and then it was summer and it was hot. I could see the cold and the hot and the cold and the hot—winters and summers and winters and summers breaking down the rocks until they were sand. Finally there was a tree growing there. I saw it grow to be an adult, and then finally it fell. In Tiwa the tree is called *tslah-ah-nay*, which means greatness. When it fell, I realized that that's how the land was imbued with greatness. This first tree awakened the memory of greatness, because it is the essence of greatness. When it hit the ground, and as it started to rot, it gave us time. The rings in the tree tell us that time expands out from a single point. It doesn't expand inwardly — not in this dimension, anyhow. Time begins with a seed of light, but once it goes out, it doesn't go back to the point of light until it breaks up into soil as humus. Then it goes back into the one, into the beginning. You can look at a stump or a cross-section of a tree and see how an insight might happen, beginning with a seed or a single flash of light and traveling out from there.

The ancient traditionalists used to use trees for ceremony. In the ceremonies they would dance around a tree or climb a tree or hang things in it, or dance back and forth as we do in the sun dance. The tree is a symbol of how time is expanding and how we are expanding as a part of that greatness or expansion. It is the symbol of the movement and expansion of Divine Thought or Divine Essence. The tree is the most concrete substance that we can see and touch that connects us to how greatness is expanding.

So, after the seeding takes place, then there is *existence*—All-that-is. The most elementary forms of life appear, the fungus appears, then other plants and other forms of life. I saw this unfolding very rapidly in my vision.

Also in my vision I saw the mountain form, and the flow of water from the mountain to our village, to Picuris. The mountain is the heart center, because water flows from the mountain top in streams and rivers, like the arteries coming away from the heart.

I saw the rivers going to Picuris, then I saw a place southwest of the center of the village. There was a crack and I was taken there, and then I was looking at it, and then, in the next instant, people appeared.

First, there was nothing, then the earth cracked open and a gaslike substance came out, and there appeared a group of people, maybe sixteen of them, standing there. They were already there, but now I saw them. They were Indian people, Native American people, with bows and arrows like the grandfathers. Three or four were elders, and there were young men and women, and then children eight or nine years old, and maybe a baby or two.

According to my vision, the beings came down

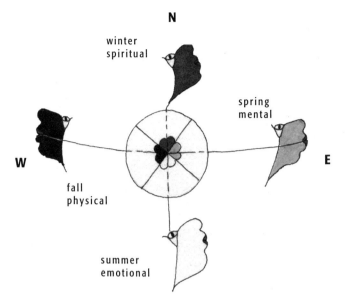

from the southeast, then they landed at the blue stone. Then, the earth formed and the waters receded and the mountains rose up, all very rapidly in my vision, though it must have taken millennia in reality. Then in the next instant, a crack appeared to the southwest of the center of the village, and the cloud appeared out of the crack. And when it cleared, the people were standing there.

I think it is important that they appeared in the southwest, for in Native American thought, the direction of the southwest is another gateway or sacred transition point. It is the same as that instant in which summer becomes fall.

There is a continuum that is the line that goes from northeast to southwest on the medicine wheel. This line, or axis, divides the All-that-is into the male and female. Along this axis, the people are separated into the winter people and the summer people. This line separates the autumn and winter on one half and the spring and summer on the other.

On this axis, in the northeast is where the black and white kachina beings landed. The northeast is the place where winter becomes spring. The winter is when things are in the womb, and spring is when they are born as idea, so the northeast is the time of seeding. Then, the idea which is seeded goes around the wheel through spring and into the summer and to that point where summer becomes autumn. That's when it is born as material reality. That's when the energy has "cooked" and what was seeded as idea takes material form.

The winter is the place of inspiration—states of inspiration. But what is interesting is that inspiration occurs not in that space which is to the north—or in the wintertime. That is not when inspiration happens. It happens right when winter ceases to exist. There is an instant when inspiration stops and spring occurs. On the intersection of two slices of light—at that line—it happens. A new idea enters, moves sun-wise through springtime into summertime and then, when it passes midsummer into autumn, it physically appears. This appearance happens at the instant when summer becomes fall, or in the southwest. Here it "falls" into material reality. Then it matures when it gets to true west. Then it goes to the north where it is infused with spirit, with the fullness of inspiration, moving sun-wise around the medicine wheel.

In my vision, the beings landed from outer space right on that slice of light between winter and spring, and thus between the spiritual and the mental realms, that place where they intersect. That intersection is the beginning of the idea. The inspiration is formed above, then it "springs" forth as idea.

Remember that at the beginning of physical manifestation, there was a crack on the earth. This is because the kachinas, or beings from outer space, came bringing power, energy. They *became* this energy and they permeated the whole planet. They landed in the southeast, and in the southwest is where they materialized. They materialized out of nothing. In the material realm I saw them land in the southeast and they became an energy that was about three feet off the ground and they looked black and white like kachinas.

Black and white represents a mental energy. (White is the house of the shattering light, and black is breath, blowing breath.) They were at first mental forms, and then in the southwest they became people who in my eyes looked like native people.

Before they were native people, however, when they were here as kachinas, they landed in a transparent ship and the next thing I knew, the land was going through a transfiguration. This transfiguration is important because when an idea descends into consciousness, it comes down and it goes into the infinite Self and it materializes and goes through a transfiguration. All the patterns are now changed. Something new has been added.

Then, maybe six billion years happened, as the earth was forming. It took that long for it to occur in linear time, in material time. In timelessness it was a split second. Then the people just appeared out of the core of the earth.

In this way, the original idea became physical; that is how powerful it was. At that instant I saw that the kachinas had seeded the whole earth.

Millennia passed and people appeared. "People" means vibration, in metaphor. The language that was spoken at Picuris, then, was already seeded in the earth, so when we ate from a garden on Picuris land we were actually eating the energy that would identify our culture, identify our speech or our world view, based on what we were eating from the land that had been seeded with energy. The energy looked like soil, or it had fused itself to become soil. But soil is also the infinite Self—*naa-meh-nay*—the Self in a state of movement, creating a greater clarity of the relationship between the physical and spiritual realms.

So what we are really interested in is how it is that we are constantly in a state of creativity, what we're creating, how we're co-creating. We are interested in how an individual cell creates by splitting itself. The cell occurs first in the northeast, and then it travels. Maybe it takes a fraction of a second or maybe it takes a day, or two days or five days. Then it splits when it gets to the southeast, and now you have two separate cells. This splitting is what caused us to separate ourselves from ourselves. It is right in the biological makeup of the consciousness of matter. In order to reproduce, life had to split itself. The split is also the way we split ourselves from our memory of ourselves, and yet it's also the way that we become ourselves.

That is the reason we have to keep rivers pure and clean, because rivers are our direct way of remembering how to reconnect ourselves to the heart. They flow from the mountain top, which is the heart center. Today we go skiing and go to the top of the mountain to reconnect ourselves to the heart. Moses went to the top of the mountain and he brought down the law of what is right, of what is connected to the heart.

At the heart center, we perceive that we are not really split. We appear to be split, but our split exists only in the material realm where perception rules our reality. But this reality is constantly changing, for perception is impermanence.

Ceremonies, like the dances we do, are to help us perceive in this impermanent, perceptual, material realm the reality of the spiritual. People respond to the ancient ceremonies because these realities are in our memory banks.

All visions are always present. A vision is what the visionary is seeing, and what the visionary is seeing is something that now the Being is choosing to perceive. When we see visions, they enter perceptual reality. In perceptual reality, the visionary is seeing something in front of him or her that is now available to be perceived by a perceiver, who has allowed himself now to perceive.

A vision is the soul drinking light. It starts with descending light, like falling rain. The descending light is the feminine, the receptive. It is just light or undifferentiated energy. To someone perceiving the vision, it looks like a picture, or a phenomenon, but it's really just the action of the soul drinking light. The visionary transformation happens in the act of perception. The soul, or consciousness, or the vast Self is drinking light that looks like awareness. It looks like receptivity; it has the quality of "as-above-so-below." It has the quality of "heaven is here now." What you want to achieve is here now, ready, given. Earth is fused with it; therefore, we can materialize it now and make it real.

That light is innocence. Everything is now open to learning; everything is now open to curiosity. Now we have the potential of creating from it what it can be or wants to be. Now we are given the energy. The vision gives the perceiver the energy — physical energy as well as mental, emotional, and spiritual energy. "Do it!"

Above all, the vision connects the personal self to the vast Self. In fact, it's all simply the vast Self *seeing*, making something perceptual because it is going to materialize it. Without materializing, matter can't exist. Without materializing, the land can't exist — the land, which is a metaphor of the vast Self.

You see, the vast Self is total nothingness. Nothing. The earth is simply a concretized, slowed-down energetic being that ended up material. What the vastness sees is what it creates. But, because it is creating what it is seeing, that vast seeing that it's doing is creating a lot of interrelationships — interconnectedness, and relationship connections. Perception does that by its very nature. Perception is a connector, a linker. Everything is linked to everything else. Hence the storytellers tell of Spider Woman weaving the web of life. All these ideas tie into the reality that there is a Seer seeing everything. We call it God, the higher power, or whatever. It is simply the vast Self seeing itself creating itself.

In my mind, however, I see a transparent ship come down with two beings, and they have white and black stripes, and these two kachinas are wizards. This vibration, then, seeds the land and the sky.

This power that lands from the up above, which appears as two beings in my vision, has

several attributes. One is the ability to fall—
"topple-ability." It is able to topple. It is able to
fall. The attribute of falling came from the heavens,
not from the earth.

It also gives us the freezing capacity, to freeze
everything in place. We can conceptualize now,
can harden. But we don't want to stop the energy
at the level of the cold, rational idea. It needs to
move through us or we ourselves get locked into
that crystallization in the intellect. We act from
fear and we become resistant to new ideas.

I tell my students that if they are stuck, if they
are resistant to new ideas or authority or
whatever, there's a meditation they can do to get
rid of that resistance. Bring some light down
through the top of the brain, then through the
heart, and then on down through the bottoms of
the feet, into the earth. What this does is connect
upper, middle, and lower brain with inner self, and
with the vast Self. Then, bring the light energy
back up through feet, through the heart, through
the brain, and back out to connect to all the
heavenly planes.

You see, one of the primary struggles in
human consciousness is the resistance to change.
Resistance is about changing crystallization to
something opposite. We tend to get stuck in the
forms. We get an idea and then five minutes later
we want to keep it alive forever. We need to let
go so a new idea can come in.

An idea comes in totally cold, freezing, from

the up-above world. It has to go through heart to ground to infinite vastness in the earth, then back up through the heart. When the energy goes back through the heart the second time, it now has heart energy — feeling, emotion. It goes to the top of the brain, then it's ready. We can now present the idea in a more balanced way.

It is when we don't connect ideas to the infinite vastness and the heart in this way that we have wars. We are stuck in cold reason, and we act from self-righteousness and fear. But when, through meditation and ceremony, we bring that cold intellectual energy down through the heart center, connect it with the vast Self, and then bring it back through the heart to the brain, we can now act from the heart, from love.

We make that connection with meditation and ceremony.

Ceremony is to awaken our memory of how we are connected with the earth or the vast Self. Many of our ceremonies are done on a seasonal basis, once a year, so that we reinstill in everybody that knowledge, reawaken that ancient process by which the heart and the mind create balance on this material plane.

The planet is made in the same perspective as the human brain because we are a product of the earth, of the geography in which we live. In terms of the brain, the top, or cerebrum of the brain is winter. The lower, inner part, or thalamus, is the summer. The energy has to descend from the top

the winter/summer people

of the brain to the inner part of the brain. It has to fall, to connect with the heart and the vast Self. When it falls and then returns again through the heart and brain, then we have creation.

The top is the mind and the bottom is the heart of the brain. The top is winter and the bottom, or heart of the brain is the summer.

Thus we have the summer/winter dialogue. At my pueblo, all the people are divided into summer people and winter people. If your mother is a summer person, then you are a summer person. If your mother is a winter person, then you are a winter person. Summer people live down at the heart of the village, while winter people have their homes up around the village on the hillsides.

At my pueblo, you always belong to your mother's clan, rather than to your father's clan. If your mother came from the Water Clan and your father came from the Eagle Clan, then you belong to the Water Clan and the *little* Eagle Clan, but you always belong more to your mother's side than you do to your father's side. I think it is because the descending feminine energy precedes the existence of the male.

Thus, if your mother was a winter person, you would be a winter person, too. You would be part of the vibration of *chi*, or the intellect. If you were a summer person, you would have the vibration of *maa*, or the heart. At Picuris, we do ceremonies to balance those energies.

In modern technological society we are unbalanced, with too much *chi* energy. We think with the head or intellect, and then articulate with the heart. But the intellect is judgmental. When we act from the intellect, we act from a base of fear. What we need to do now is to think with the heart and articulate with the head. The heart just wants to love, so that when we are directed from the heart, we act from a base of love.

In order to clear our brains of judgment, we should stand on our heads. We should reverse our usual way of thinking. Instead of sending ideas directly out from the rational brain, we would move the energy into the earth, and receive vibrations directly into the brain from the earth, which is the vastness of the vast Self. The brain would send them up through the heart, up the legs to the clouds and sky — to be articulated in purity.

The rational mind says that whatever it cannot understand is not real, and that misconception is what separates us from God. Thus, when we create in technological society, we get in trouble, because the brain thinks, "I am better than God, I am better than the natural world." It thinks that the only things it can bring into existence are those things it understands; whatever doesn't have meaning to the rational brain is not appropriate. That's okay, because that is how we find out we have to give it up — to let go and let God.

Eventually, we have to go back to God. We have to go back to our faith, to our religion, to our belief, and back to ourselves. I am not saying that we need to start a religion or anything; it just means that we have to go back to love, back to the Self, and then we are truly creating from that space of devotion, of worship.

Let's not take this out of context and decide, now that we know this, that everything is going to be all right because we have figured it all out. Life is not about figuring things out. It is about realizing that everything is unfolding in a very natural way. Eventually, those principal ideas will manifest in material, perceptual reality, and new things will have become possible on earth.

Remember, life is movement. It is *nay*. It is manifesting placement which connects us with the new thing that has now entered. In other words, we move into a relationship with the new thing that is coming into form. We move up a notch.

I think what we are doing in this plane, actually, is that we are remembering how we became perfect through materialization. After all, this material plane is perceptual in nature. In reality, there is no time; it happens all at once. Time is only perceptual. We have broken it down in pieces of time so we could perceive it. We are curious and we want to experience it. It's just like being in a story.

In my vision I saw the different eternities in which we operate. I saw it all as a beehive. It looked like a mound, like a cone. Each cell where the honey is stored is an eternity. There are all these bees flying around, saying, "beeeeee, beeeee." We are in a state of "bee"ing-ness in this eternity. Each of these cells or circles is a memory that we are recalling right now. But when we finish, we want to go to the next circle, then to the next circle, and the next circle. We are going to be here forever!

All that memory is, is how the heart is remembering. We are remembering how the heart experienced fear to become whole, how the heart experienced separation to become whole. Because the only way it wanted to do it was through illusion. So the heart is the great being, the great mystery. All that is here now is a reflection of a being who lies in a state of dreaming and is perceiving, in reflection, what already is.

To help us perceive the process by which creation takes place, we might imagine this *waa,* inspiration, or life energy falling down from the noosphere. In its falling, this *waa* energy is pure female energy, full of potential. The instant it hits the biosphere, the instant it is stopped, it is transformed to male energy.

Now, this energy begins to move around and upward in a spiral. It splits, part of it spiraling sunwise, or clockwise, and part of it spiraling moonwise, or counterclockwise. And in these sunwise and moonwise spiraling motions, it forms the medicine wheel.

The falling energy enters at the northeast. As it hits the core energy of the biosphere, a new movement is awakened. Until the feminine energy enters, the core energy is lying down, asleep. The feminine awakens it. Now it is a new masculine, spiritual energy, spiraling upward.

Part of the awakened energy becomes intellectual, or *"chi"* energy, and moves clockwise. It spirals east as undifferentiated idea. Then it moves to the south, where it becomes emotion and learns its place within all that is. Now it begins to dance its dance or sing its song. Then it spirals on to the west, where it becomes physical. The dancing emotional energy takes on pattern and this pattern is its physical form. Then it spirals on to the north where it receives a redoubling of spirit and lifts. This is the clockwise movement of the energy, the intellectual, or left-brain movement.

At the same time, part of the energy moves counterclockwise, or moonwise. This is the spiritual or *"maa"* energy. From the northeast, it spirals to the north, where the energy receives a new infusion of spirit, which lifts it. Then it moves to the west, where it takes on pattern or physical form. Then it moves to the south, takes its place in relation to all that is, and begins to dance as emotion, then it moves to the east where it is purified as idea. This moonwise movement of energy is the spiritual, right-brain movement.

The spiraling energies form a double helix that lifts. Now the All-that-is can express a higher purpose, a fuller awareness. Perhaps this is why the ear of corn is so sacred to native people. Corn provides the image of the double helix in the way the kernels of corn are arranged around the corn cob. The Puebloans believe that first woman and first man came from the corn, from a male/female stalk of corn.

The spiraling energies, sunwise and moonwise, form a double helix, lifting. As they lift, the consciousness of the individual is pushed upward. What was formerly not possible becomes possible. A higher level is attained. This higher level now becomes the new ground of consciousness, and the process begins again. More new ideas are received from the feminine life energies that fall from the noosphere. These energies enter the medicine wheel at the northeast, spiral in the double helix, manifest, materialize, spiritualize and lift the consciousness still higher.

This is the movement of the perfection of consciousness.

All ceremony is about this process, this breathing in and spiraling of energies sunwise and moonwise. All ceremony is designed to enhance this process and bring about the perfection of consciousness.

inspiration

life is made of breath, matter, and movement.

One of the qualities of inspiration is awareness. When we are inspired, awareness appears in the psyche of our being. At the moment when inspiration occurs, a new consciousness fuses itself with the personal self. Inspiration is coming from the inifinte Self and it fuses itself with the personal self. This is a physical thing. It happens in the physical body, in the flesh.

Then, heaven comes onto earth. In that instant, the below and the above come together. Now you have connection to all of the heavens, and there is a flow of energy that wasn't there before.

That energy fuses itself to the heart, to the center of that of consciousness. Now loving attention flows. The emotions are involved. Celebration occurs.

Immediately there's awareness again. This second awareness substantiates the original awareness. The original awareness came just to the self, to the mind. Now the heart is involved and the heart and the mind are one in awareness.

At that point the inspiration creates a flood of light — a radiance. This is what creates that ecstasy. "Ah! I've been inspired! I have an idea!"

After that "Eureka!" moment of celebration, you have the bonding. In that instant, the inspiration connects itself to everything. It creates a whole. It connects the heavens and the earth and it creates empowerment.

Once again, in the moment when inspiration appears in the psyche of being, awareness fuses itself with the self, the self fuses itself with the heart, the heart fuses itself with awareness. Awareness creates a radiance, a sense of light, of knowing. It creates linkages and fuses itself to a sense of relativity with everything else. Everything is placed in its proper perspective.

Heaven and earth come together. There's no longer up above and down below. They become one.

Inspiration comes with the inhalation, not the exhalation. Also, I think inspiration is a close relative of oxygen. I notice that when they put the oxygen on in the airplane just before we're going to land, I have my best ideas.

The understanding of inspiration comes with an understanding of the physicality of breathing. If you want inspiration, stop thinking. Thinking will block the process. Instead, forget what you're trying to do and just breathe.

Actually, true inspiration comes when we *aren't* breathing. True inspiration comes when we don't exist. It comes when we momentarily disappear from being.

In order for inspiration to bring about creative

action, there must be purity, placement, awareness, innocence, and carrying.

Purity is the process by which the heart uses the art of struggle to achieve awareness of its relationship to the vast Self. Purity then takes that vast infinite awareness and connects it to the personal self. This crystallized thought or personal awareness, can now be used as the key to unlock the gate between the physical, knowing world and the spiritual (breath) plane. The breath, or spiritual world, is the world from which inspiration appears. Inspired thought, or an idea, comes as cognizance or understanding to the thinking mind. Now it can be formulated into an impulse for a creative action.

We have the idea of one vast inifinte Self awareness and the idea of a personal finite awareness, and then we have the process by which these two awarenesses interact.

Think of a circle. Everything outside the circle is the vast infinite awareness that is undefined because it is in the "no-form place," and it is not knowable at this stage to the individual person. Everything inside the circle is that which is already known to the individual and is the current ongoing reality of the person, his beliefs, values, and attitudes. In the process of interaction new wisdom enters as a mental form from the vast inifinte Self into the circle of the personal self.

Infinite vastness enters the circle at the east as mental impulse. As the mental impulse comes, it

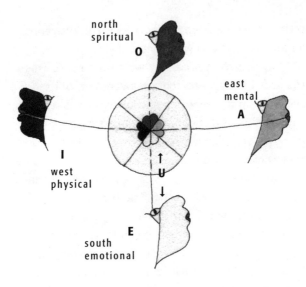

ignites and awakens an emotion. (It moves to the south on the medicine wheel.) Next it expresses itself as a physical impulse (i.e., moves to the west), and finally as an inspiration of spiritual wisdom (north). As it circles, it completes its journey in the inner psyche of the personal self, at which time it formulates itself into an idea to be acted upon.

Through the action of movement in this process, the individual materializes or brings forth into the perceivable world a new clarity of inspired knowing.

the medicine wheel

*t*he medicine wheel contains the five principal vibrations or ideas that are in the five vowel sounds:

East = **A** = purification

South = **E** = placement

West = **I** = awareness

North = **O** = childlike innocence

Vertical (up and down) = **U** = carrying

The purpose of *purification* is to clear out all types of pollution. One practice is breathing. In the breath, you give life to all the forms being created in you. In exhalation, you clear them back into formlessness. The exhalation — the out-breath — is the pollution cleanser.

In chanting, you will be owning your forms and then discharging them within the rhythm of breathing in and out. You breathe in (own your forms) and breathe out (let them go).

Chanting, then, is a rite of purification. There are many forms of purification rites in various cultures. The traditional sweat lodge is a purification ceremony. Catholics go to confession and receive absolution and Holy Communion. Other Christians have similar purification rites in connection with Holy Communion. Even jogging is a purification rite, because when we jog, we sweat.

We jog to run off fat or to run off our problems.

Purification ceremonies help us humans to deal with our fears, both imagined and real.

Placement gives us a spot on the planet in which to exist. Placement deals both with location and with what we do and believe. Placement is important, because at a certain level of consciousness, we do not exist.

What is placement's function in our lives on the spiritual path? First, we are on a spiritual path, whether or not we are conscious of this. Everything on planet earth is alive with breath and is spiritual by its very nature. Placement gives us a way by which to focus ourselves on the life that surrounds us.

We practice placement by focusing on the place on which we stand. When you are ready to deal with a current situation in life, sit or stand still. Stop all physical motion. During that moment of placement, your focus brings clarity.

We may place ourselves in a physical geography, or on a landscape of philosophical leanings.

Placement brings us new potential. In the moment of placement, we are whole, complete with crystallized knowing. Now something is comprehensible to us. Now there is more than enough psychic energy to enjoy the satisfaction of our completed realization, and more than enough energy to carry out the idea.

The word understanding is a good example of

this state because it carries within it the idea of placement. When we understand a concept, we literally stand under it. Our placement connects the creative insight from above with the ground, with our material, physical world.

Creativity is symbolized by:

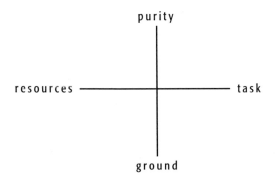

This symbol represents both creativity and caretaking of the land — the land which is made of the vast Self.

The vertical line symbolizes realization, the coming into form of the new creation. The new creation is based on unconditional love in a state of inspiration. The horizontal line symbolizes the level we're on as we're moving upward toward purity and clarity. We are given a task and resources to help us move upward. One of the resources we are given is our physical bodies. Our mental, emotional and spiritual bodies are the tasks we achieve through our physical bodies.

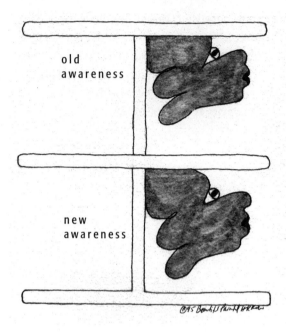

old
awareness

new
awareness

©95 ...

We're creating mental, emotional and spiritual bodies as we go higher and higher toward purity and clarity.

In this symbol, placement is both at the horizontal line and at the bottom of the vertical line, connected with the earth.

This is the symbol of doing or action, as well as knowing. Our original beliefs or values become the foundation for new awareness.

New *awareness* annihilates our most recent level of knowledge so that we can become aware of the next higher level of knowing. We cannot leave our current level of understanding until we let go of it, and we can only do that when the unexpected occurs and we are surprised into new awareness. It is in this process of unexpected knowingness that the old knowledge we were attached to dies. Now the new awareness can come into being.

One of our passionate attachments is to what we currently know. As with jealousy, anger, greed, pride, and the other passions, our attachment to what we know is a mental obscuration which blocks our ability to learn and grow. We are attached to our latest knowing until new knowing arrives.

Innocence is to seek awareness, to surrender completely to infinite vastness and to ask for the self-imposed limitations to be removed so that teachability can happen. Innocence is made up of three vibrations:

1. The vibration of being in search of awareness or self-knowing.

2. The vibration of the search process itself.

3. The vibration of crying for a vision so that beauty may be found.

Carrying is initiation. At sunrise, the sun's light initiates the day. At sundown, the sunlight initiates the night by ending the light of the day and beginning the dark of night. Similarly, life is carrying all that is; all plants, animals, and things. Life initiates us into linear time. We live from one moment to the next one. We live inside each

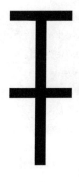moment, then it passes on so that we can become something new.

A past moment that just died carries and becomes the foundation for the new knowing that was just born.

Our ancient ancestors help us carry our new knowing because they return to us from the infinite vastness that looks like land here on earth.

ceremonies of dance

*i*n the creation myth when we were created as life, we came from the black light into the white light. The black light is light that is in a state of motion, in a state of blowing darkness. Blowing blackness, or blowing breath, is both breath and matter. (Remember that God means breath, matter, and movement.)

We reconnect ourselves with our source by doing a long dance in which we dance in a circle throughout an entire night. For half the night we dance sunwise (clockwise) and then we turn and for the rest of the night we dance moonwise (counterclockwise). The long dance is performed at night because the night light is symbolically the "blackness" or black matter, whereas the long dancer is the symbol of the "blowing" (moving) aspect of blowing darkness.

Again, symbolically, the long dancers are the blowing as they dance in the dark blackness of the nighttime light. Additionally, the long dance is performed at night because the dark spaces between the stars are our origin, our symbol of birth into this life. And as the dancers look into the night sky they know intuitively, through their genetic makeup, that that is true. The black light is how matter and the breath are together in the act of materializing different shades of light (dark to light).

The blowing is the breath.

Matter is black light that has been changed into white light so it can be seen as lighted stars or as materialized forms on this planet. The movement part of breath, matter, and movement is the slowing down, the cooling, of the blowing blackness into physical crystallized solids that make up the starry night.

We, as humans, are slowed down (cooled down) energy that has crystallized us into ideas that came from the blowing blackness. We, as humans, will have tendencies to get stuck in the forms that we create because it is in our nature to do so. It is in our nature because we are made of energy that has the potential to be a liquid, solid, or gas. We become moon-sun dancers, long dancers or drum dancers to break the crystallization— to unstick ourselves from our self-imposed limitations.

We were made in the same way or image as the earth was made by blowing blackness. Consequently, when we dance we do it for the earth as well as for our personal selves. And this is how we serve the earth.

Today we know, because astronomers tell us, that a supernova made the original elements that make up the earth and those who inhabit the earth. The supernova that created our planet came to create our galaxy long before our sun was made. It is told in a Tiwa prayer:

"We came from the night time
Into the daytime,
And they carry us as
The People."

In dancing we move from our crystallizations that keep us imprisoned. As our bodies move in the dance, we momentarily disappear. Upon our return in the next instant, we arrive with a greater clarity of our senses and feelings. We connect to a resurgence of vitality, physically as well as emotionally. Our inner organs begin to breathe with less and less effort, mental blocks are released. Our psyches can now redefine them and assist in the restructuring of the newly claimed self.

As we release mental, emotional, physical, and spiritual blocks, we sense and feel beauty—beauty in ourselves and in all beings in life. We have successfully connected the personal self to the radiance of Divine Beauty. The expansion that has been created allows us next to have new inspirations for new challenges in life, and we begin to see problems in our personal life as opportunities for growth, rather than obstructions.

ceremony and the essence of
material forms

One of the first things I learned while at
Picuris is that everything is alive.
Everything, every form, has a center—
its own personal resonance, its own
heart. And that is the way it stays connected, by
its own identifiable resonance. That's how it
determines its essence and keeps its form. Thus, a
plum tree produces plums, a cherry tree produces
cherries.

The sun gives the plants energy made of
inspiration, and this way they stay alive. The plants
stay alive by breathing. They breathe in sunlight,
and through photosynthesis they process it. That
is how they produce their energies, their fruits.

Energy is constantly moving. The sun dancer
knows this from breathing in and breathing out
through the hollow bone. After a while, by virtue
of doing this hundreds of times, and through years
of practice, we learn that our breathing in and out
is the same as the energy going from the earth up
to the sky and back down to the earth, up to the
sky and back down again.

At Picuris, they use the pole climb to show
the same thing. In the pole climb, they go up the
pole to get the things that are waiting at the top,
and then they come down. Another example is
the vertical line of the Christian cross. This ability

to move up and down is an attribute that we get from the sun. This up-and-down-flowing energy bonds whatever is near with whatever is far away. It connects the finite with the infinite in this process of movement up and down.

When the finite self is connected to the inifinite self, then the soul comes in. Soul is like the soil that gives sunlight a place to put down roots. Sunlight roots itself in soil, so that the plant can grow to its greatest quality. It gives some roots into the ground and it gives a sense of purity and clarity.

There is the dialog between the light and no-light, between day and night.

The daylight, philosophically, is the rational mind; everything that is knowable is light. Everything that is rational, that can be understood, has this clarity of the sunlight. The night is the creative.

The soil gives the plant the gift of manifestation, of movement, so that it can bond to the heavens. It is stuck in the ground with roots and it grows upward toward the sun, and in that process it is going up toward the heavens and bonding with them. Should that plant be in poor soil, it will not produce its highest potential. This also applies to the human condition. If we don't place ourselves in the rich soil of life that is nourishing to us, we may not achieve our potential.

When the Picuris people heard about the

explosion of an atom bomb at Hiroshima, we performed a ceremony to bring about peace. We took all the implements of war from the village and buried them in the ground. The reason that we take a powerful instrument and stick it in the ground is to send it back to its origin, to the inifinte self. The finite is the weapon, the infinite is the earth. So we send it back. And when we send it back that way, something happens psychically to the planet and to the object. It returns to innocence — back to the Self — just like the image in the Bible of beating swords into plowshares. When we place something in the ground, the energy of that object reverts. In this case, war-making, hostile energy reverts to an energy of compassion.

The Picuris people, when they buried the weapons of war, were taking care of the earth. They see theirs as a role of caretaking. Caretaking is what the shepherds were doing when Jesus was born.

When you put something in the ground, when you bury anything, it returns to the dream. When you bury a rifle, it returns back to the dream, before it was dreamt into rifleness, for the purposes of injury, of killing.

Material Forms

Crystallized forms, such as rocks, hold the energy of their connections to the upper planes, to the noosphere, where inspiration comes from.

They also carry the capacity to radiate energy. This energy wants to help the personal self as well as the inifinte self by moving all things to climb. This energy asks to ascend; it moves things higher.

Everything, even the hard rock, is alive. Nothing is really inanimate. When you fast for days without food or water, you see the rock is really buzzing with life. Each rock is different. You can see the difference and you know which rock is a heart rock, which rock is lung rock, which is a walking rock. It's not that you just pick up an ordinary rock and say, "This is a heart rock." Each rock resonates with a principal idea of oneness, heartness, sittingness, or walkingness. Each rock talks to you and it tells you what it is.

Ordinary life is continually talking to us, but we eat too much salt and too much sugar. Salt in your body steals your light. It robs you of your capacity to see psychically. You are less able to perceive accurately and quickly, and to comprehend what is perceived. When the salt level drops, it creates a resonance of craving, a vacuum, that calls to it light. I've been doing sweat lodges for forty years, and I know from personal experience that I can see better when my body is low on salt.

Sugar makes our blood cry. It gives us a craving and makes us jittery. We have no peace. We're too well fed, too full, too comfortable to hear life talking to us. We lose our capacities to connect. In fasting, we go back to the guiding advice of ordinary life, and we can learn from everyday things like stones, leaves, the bark of a tree, the bark of a dog.

One of the things the rock wants to do, one of its jobs, is to create linkages, connecting us not just to the finite, but to the infinite, the essence of our beingness. Because we are infinite.

Of course, we are also finite. We can take a microscope and look down into the cells of our own bodies. That is the finite. But we are also part of the vastness of an infinite universe. I tried traveling the universe once and discovered that it went on for millions and millions and millions of light years. Actually it is round, like a beehive that goes on forever. Each one of its cells or circles is an eternity.

The universe is a whole philosophical perspective of the understanding. It is a vast working model of how the unfolding of consciousness is occurring, so that we have a cognitive as well as a creative resonance or image. This unfolding of consciousness is occurring on the micro as well as the macro scale, so that every single action that is taken, whether it is mental, emotional, physical or spiritual, is in dialog with this presence, with this understanding of cosmic truth.

climbing   In Tiwa we say *we-leh-who*, which means to climb upward. Remember every single word in Tiwa has multiple meanings; it's not just one thing. To the ordinary person in Picuris, when we say, *we-leh-who*, that means "we climb upward." *We-leh-who* also means to give oneself totally and completely to the process that is ongoing, in childlike innocence. *We-leh-who* means we are in a place of no judgment or control. We are not thinking about what is going to happen; we are totally innocent. We are teachable at that point. We are emptiness.

Leh means we become the essence of peace, the tool of peace, of connection to the vertical light of the vast Self moving upward.

We use the word *leh-leh,* which means belt. *Leh* means the "belt of peace." (That's where the wampum belt comes from.) Imagine a belt around my middle. I want to slip that belt up to a higher chakra. The word, the sound vibration *lay,* is there. It means you bring the belt from the lower chakra up, for new understanding.

A belt is not just to keep your clothes on. The belt line area of the physical anatomy of the human being is telling us to move higher. When someone used the word *leh-leh* at Picuris, that used to tell us, "You slouch. There is no reason why you have to walk as if you were walking down a blind alley anymore. You can be enlightened. You can know that a belt is more than a belt." So the second meaning, the fuller understanding of this belt, is that it is to give us purity, higher clarity. It is the potential to connect the personal self to the pathway between that which is physical and that which is spiritual. So now we can cross freely back and forth between where we happen to be physically at this moment in time and space and where God is. God can feed us inspiration because we have a corridor, a pathway. It's like the hollow bone, where energy comes through freely, up and down, and gives us enlightenment.

The interesting thing about this realm, this corridor, is that it is open only for a short time, maybe a split second, or maybe three seconds or five seconds. Then it shuts down again and waits for you to apply yourself mentally, emotionally, physically, or spiritually. Or, more likely, you apply yourself in all those ways because they tend to happen together. Through effort, the self goes back up to the top and it opens up, gets more inspiration, then brings this inspiration back down again.

When I talk about how we are learning to be, I sometimes put it in terms of the equidistant cross. When we are at the bottom of the cross, we are like water. We flow to the lowest place, we find the lowest common denominator.

Now, as soon as we apply effort, we begin to lift ourselves up until we reach up to the highest potential. That is the only time when we truly exist. That is when we are having impact, when we are contributing something to humanity.

The rest of the time we are being in the normal vibration which is in the middle, or maybe we are not even reaching that. We're basically kind of lazy, but through effort we move ourselves to normalcy, which is the middle, and then as we go up higher, we are better and better and better, but we're still not at our fullest potential.

Our fullest potential comes when we get a flash of light. We reach a peak experience at which point we've broken through to a new level of being, a new level of understanding, a new level of cognizance, a new level of awareness. We have touched the source of our inspiration, the source that has given the physical body life.

Think of a cross with a horizontal bar and a vertical bar. The horizontal bar is the personal self. That's the rational self that says, this is what life is, all the different forms. "I had better not walk in front of a moving car, I might get run over." That's the personal self. Now, the vertical cross is the vast Self. As the horizontal bar moves up, it's being fed by the heavenly planes which are out to the left and the right of the vertical bar. These heavenly planes are feeding the consciousness with inspiration. The self is fed, but not yet enlightened. The only time it is enlightened is when it has achieved its true potential through effort. That's when a light comes on and you feel totally washed with light.

fasting   Fasting has always been used to enhance this process: to enhance faith, to clarify our thinking about doctrine or values, and thus to increase belief. How does this work on the vibrational level?

First of all, in its original state, the energy that creates all form — concrete or abstract — is rapidly moving light energy. This energy slows down to a crawl so that it becomes matter. The light slows to become physical forms — atoms and molecules. Inside matter, however, imagine that the energy remains moving, now in slow motion, just barely in a state of movement, so that it can't be perceived by the human at all.

When the person fasts, his psychic energy begins to speed up, evoking precognitive dreams, premonitions, or instructive visionary experiences. By speeding up the psychic flow of energy, fasting increases the energy of the normal human intelligence, giving birth to a new awareness. The old pattern changes, changing the behavior of the person.

Faith is enhanced in three ways. First there remains an increased awareness that was not there before, and because of this a pattern has changed. Secondly, a greater freedom is experienced. Third, there is a renewed interest in one's life, an increased desire to contribute to life, which is the essence of faith.

In summary, fasting changes the slow-moving flow of the person's human intelligence and speeds it up to a rapid pace, which allows for paranormal experiences and enhanced faith.

Rapidly moving light energy is the hunter, stalking knowledge. *Chueh-lo* is speed in Tiwa. *Chueh-lo* hunts and captures the form that is to be rooted or placed.

Pii-aah-saah is slow motion in Tiwa. Slow motion places and roots life as form. Slowly moving light energy — matter on the physical level — is constantly being purified with heart energy.

movement   In Tiwa, goodness and movement are synonymous.

Fasting, prayer, and meditation are incorporated in some movement or action — good action. Many of the ancient mystic schools, monasteries of ancient times, encouraged fasting and prayer, because the basis for reaching one's highest potential is prayerful meditation, which is a spiritual movement.

Now movement is also what gives us the capacity to perceive. Without movement it is as if we have been born without eyes. We have no eyes to see with and no inner eye — the third eye.

Movement is an essential part of Godness on this plane of reality, because God is breath, matter, and movement. Without movement, there cannot be creation in matter. Without movement, the breath cannot instill creativity. It is that movement that helps us see that we can create the next thing. Without movement, we can't see what is being created. And that is why we have materialization into form — so that we can see. Seeing, perceptual reality, and material form are the same.

placement Everything in the natural material world exists to tell us and to show us how well we are doing.

For instance, *cha* is the tree. *Cha* is also the now, *cha* is life's chant, *cha* is the tree of life and *cha* is greatness. If you were to fast seven or eight days, as soon as you touch a tree or you sit on it or lean on it, it's going to tell you how much greatness is there. That is in the vibration, *cha*. That vibration might tell you you could be doing better. It might tell you to consider your age and the effort you're putting into life. It might also teach you how you can continue to keep yourself in greatness, because that is in its vibration.

In the same way, when you have been fasting for a few days without food or water, a heart stone is going to connect you to where your center is. It will show you the God-given gifts that you were born with, that make up your center, your resonance. Even as a plum tree produces a plum and a cherry tree produces a cherry, so you are born with the capacity to produce your own particular form of fruit. Each entity or each form has to go back to its resonance to check in, to find out what it is being. Since we are mental, emotional, physical, spiritual beings, we go back to find our placement.

That's why Native American practices are so popular today. People really want to find themselves again; they really want to find their placement, so they go to a culture that has kept these ceremonies. But we are so connected to form that we look at a dance and say, "Oh, what a great rattle. It has this horsehair on it. It has these beads on it." We get distracted from the core, resonant vibration that this ceremony is about.

The ceremony is really there to get us in touch with something in ourselves that makes up the constellation of our presence here. When we really connect to these different ceremonies — not so much to their appearance, but to their mystical resonances, their vibrations — we can get in touch with the core essence of that particular form, that particular understanding.

we-leh-who We-leh-who means to go up. We means to give. *Leh* means the horizontal plane. *Who* gives us a sense of being carried. It gives us a sense of the connection to the vastness, to the heavenly planes. *Who* means God is carrying us, or God is carrying the action that is being taken. This is connecting us to the highest potential of the heavenly planes, and it is giving us the place of childlike innocence in which we are simply conduits of energy at the core of existence— energy that is moving through us without any effort on our part and nourishing our souls.

This doorway to the core stays open only long enough to present insight, and then it closes down and waits for the next input of psychic energy. We are like strobe lights; we go off and on and off and on. Our movements, as we act out these insights through effort, create the next opening, a corridor to new insights or inspirations.

Any time we put effort into anything, it moves us up; not necessarily all the way up, but higher than we have been before. Sometimes we'll actually sense a flash of light, like something has changed. But the rest of the time we simply feel stimulated and we think it is great.

Once we become our true potential, our highest possibility, a symbolic death occurs. At this point, the persons we thought we were, and the patterns we were following, cease to exist, and then we go up. We have a new design now. We can remember what we were, but now the old patterns of human behavior are no longer impinging upon our physical activities, our mental behavior, our emotional behavior, our spiritual behavior. We have entered a whole new level of being.

walking in beauty So how do we keep ourselves open to insights? By treating ourselves and others as we would like to be treated.

In Tiwa, goodness means *co-wen*. It means the beauty of childlike innocence, loving kindness that is climbing upwards through the base self, more and more becoming new beauty. *Co-wen* in everyday speech means "all is well," but it really means all is well because what is being enhanced is beauty. All beauty wants is more beauty, and the person's attitude is right. That person is in the right place, because he is really only being beauty. That is all he chooses to be — the highest potential of beauty that he can be at this point.

Beauty is the only thing we are here for. In everything else we do, we're just trying to find beauty.

The three essentials to be in a state of beauty are:

Level 1: You have to have that connection with Oneness;

Level 2: You have to be in reflection (which is what we call duality);

Level 3: You have to be in movement.

Beauty is the action of being in the moment. In the moment, you can't just be at level number one. You have to simultaneously be on levels two and three. I think that's what they mean by the Holy Trinity, the Three-in-One.

In Tiwa, beauty is *bah-chu. Bah* is related to the legs. Let me walk; we use our legs to walk. The word *chu* means everywhere. When you are in the state of beauty, you are everywhere but nowhere. But you are in a state of movement, which is beauty that has connected to all the heavenly planes and is being carried by God. You are in a state of beatitude.

When the Native American people speak of walking in beauty, they're really saying, "Walk in love. It is the blessing way."

One of the qualities of the blessing way is the connection that we have with the people that we love, our fellow human beings. What we need to do is keep a loving bond between us. Then we realize that if we have a loving bond with plants, animals, and the land around us, as if we were in a garden and we were the gardener, then we walk in beauty, and the beauty is who we are and what we are doing. Beauty comes from our relationship to all those around us.

At the end of their prayers, the Indians say, "All my relations." That's what they're talking about. We have a bond. Bonding is one of the qualities of Beauty.

Beauty is also purity. And what is purity? Purity exists when the heart fuses with carrying. We carry each other; we carry our philosophies. That's one of the qualities of purity, an awareness that crystallizes in this radiance of inner knowing so that we can see the spiritual and the physical connection.

One of the things purity is doing in the context of beauty is crystallizing, so that we can see, so that we can feel and then have a clarity of the connection between inspiration and materialism. Beauty is seeing something that is manifesting and that's clear, has intent, has purity, and that gives us a special insight about inspiration.

The last aspect of beauty is awareness. In the true experience of beauty, awareness is total. The true experience of beauty is to disappear into those qualities that I have just spoken about. When you disappear into them, you have no desire for them. You just *are* them. That is what our prayer says when it speaks of the beauty path to the four directions.

The beatitudes of life are to celebrate how it is that we are walking here. Walking is the way we celebrate our toes, and our feet, and our legs and our backs, and our eyes, and our hands, and our arms, and all of our internal organs. Because everything is in movement. Walking in beauty is an orchestration of all of the beatitudes — the holy walk in this plane.

ah-who   Think again of the cross. When the horizontal bar is at the top of the vertical line, that is the only time we are doing anything that is worth anything. It is at the moment that we are taking a brand new action when we are reaching the highest potential. This is the moment when the old pattern dies. That is when God comes in and is involved in our actions. And we are the physical body for the translation of that energy into our next highest potential. This is the moment of transformation, for us as the actors in liaison with God's presence. And not just for us. At that moment, we are also enhancing cosmic

ah-who

consciousness. In Tiwa, we say whenever we are doing something worthwhile, we are contributing to the basic humanity of that moment in time and physical history.

The Picuris people are very intelligent beings, and I think it is because they follow this doctrine. Whether they know it or not, it is innate in their language. They say *"Ah who." Ah who* means "the breath of highest inspiration is washing us."

Tiwa is not concerned about two-leggeds, or four-leggeds, or any particular species. Its only interest is achievement of the highest potential, the highest energy level of purity, so the soul can be fed. In this way, we imprint the future and promote the evolution of unconditional love in consciousness.

The Indians signed contracts with the government to provide them with all of their needs — their social, economic, and political needs. That created a dependency. And with dependency, you don't try to excel to your highest potential. Instead of exploding to new consciousness, you begin to implode. I found in my research that dependency created a lot of alcoholism and drug abuse, because people are not happy. They are not trying to achieve their highest potential.

Again, good action takes place when God is doing the action. Any time we are doing something good, God is there, because God is the being who is achievement. Goodness comes into being through our actions. The actions that we take together with God bring us physical satisfaction and fulfill our longing for life.

Life by its very nature is a giant church made of unconditional love, a place where the soul is continually fed. Whenever you practice your highest potential, you are feeding the soul what it needs. You are keeping yourself open with inspirational thoughts. Then you feel great, and jump up and say, "Wow! This is great stuff!"

Truly, all there is in life is beauty, made of unconditional love, and everything else we do is simply a time of waiting for beauty to happen again and again.

When I say we don't exist, I mean that the only time we truly exist is when we are reaching and being our highest potential. We are at the top of the vertical bar. At any other time, we are not contributing either to ourselves or to humanity. We are simply existing. When we are simply existing, that is when we get into activities like killing each other, because we are not happy. We are not happy because we are just existing. We ask for the death of this pattern in which we are stuck so we may be reborn into the breath of inspired living.

Yet, we humans are afraid of dying. This fear arises because we are separate from the vast Self. But we have separated to find out what it means to be separate form, so that we could understand that the false code of materialism is not what God is. God is relationship to eternal life.

Yet through life in this material dimension, we carry on a dialog with materialism. This dialog automatically puts us in touch with how materialism is inspiring us to create more of what matters in our lives.

God brings two powers together—the material and the eternal. When this happens, then we can do what some people call the miraculous.

The miraculous, interestingly enough, only appears on the scene during times of emergency. During an emergency, we somehow merge that part of our separate selves back to true Self. In that moment—in that flash of light—we can manifest our true essence.

An emergency occurs when the world we

have created has collapsed. What we perceive as the "real world" is really just a collection of things we have constructed in our psyche that we understand to be reality. When that reality is shattered — in that instant — our self-assurance ends. And at that point, we truly exist.

The rest of the time, we don't exist. The rest of the time we are trying to establish that we exist.

We try to establish we exist by perpetuating our various perceptions of reality. We are afraid that if we don't, we will disappear, and that if we disappear, we will die; and that if we die, we don't exist, not realizing that we really *don't* exist. Then we give it up, and we shatter our reality in the split of the moment. Only then are we really in touch with the vast Self. Only then do we really exist.

Maybe it happens during an earthquake, when all of a sudden trees and houses are falling down, when the freeway is cracking open and swallowing cars. At that moment, you give up. Then all of a sudden, at that moment, you are out of the danger; you are way over there on the other side of the mountain. Your mind says, "Hey, what happened? I must have just thought I was in danger." No, you really were in danger, but a miracle happened automatically because destiny decided that it needed you for another week.

So, our technological mastery of the universe is proper in order to find out that it is not mastery of anything. It is mastery of self, which is not really mastery of anything. It is how we come to know that we just simply *are*.

All our efforts and technology are ways we purposefully veer away from our center. We do it because, in the expansion of the vastness, we have an innocence in us which is extremely curious. Innocence is curious, just like a little child. It wants to look at everything, and then after a while it becomes awestruck by what it sees and begins to make gods of those things.

It is so awestruck that all of a sudden the high school date is the most wonderful thing that has happened in the whole universe and — *gee!* — the lights will never end, and you've arrived in heaven and you are glad you veered away from the center to have this experience.

My Tiwa grandfather taught me that work is worship. And yet if we don't exist, and none of this exists, and there is nothing that we really need to do except know that we don't exist (except in the sense that we are part of the vast Self), why do we need to work?

We need to work because we have physical bodies, and these physical bodies are really forms that can be traced back to sacred dimensions. In perceptual, material reality, the sacred dimensions finally end up looking like a finger on a hand. In that finger, in that hand, these sacred dimensions are present, and every time we move the finger, every time we are in the state of movement, we are worshiping that finger idea. Because work is worship. By movement, or work, we keep this body strong so that we can continue worshiping that original idea of the finger, or the back, or the knees, or the feet.

The human is the microcosm of all that is contained in the macrocosm of the Vast Self.

The words given for these parts of the body in Tiwa tell us what principal ideas we are worshiping as we move and use each part. For instance, the ear in Tiwa is *tlschu*, which means *to do in order to give*. The face is *tzu*, which means *to enter*. The skin is *hai*, which means *to lift*. The head is *peh-nay*, which means *to focus*. Hair is *pah*, which means *light*. Clothing is *pii ah*, which means *to make*. The tongue is *wii-ineh*, which means *giving to awareness*. The eyes are *cheh*, which means *to cook*. The nose is *pwfu-ii*, which means *to expand*, and also *to pin onto*. The mouth is *tlscha moh*, which means *to see greatness*.

The feet are *iin*, which means *placement*. The legs are *bahh*, which means *direction*, the direction in which something is to go. Hands are *maa-nay-nay*, which means *to manifest*, or *to create*. The arms are *haah-eh*, which means *to embrace*. The body as a whole is *tu-nay*, which means *beauty*. When we work with our bodies, we are worshiping the principal idea of beauty, as well as the principal ideas of all its parts.

In order to keep worshiping, we have to keep working our bodies. Thus, we create institutions around work, and then we throw in something like money as a motivator. Whenever the human moves, whatever he does, he's already in ceremony. She's already in ceremony. Each ceremony that we perform is to help us remember the ceremony that we *are*. It is to further enhance our relationship to the vastness of who we are. We are the original cosmic plan that eventually, as it came into being, took on human form.

We are catalysts, here to bring about changes. When we walk, we are balancing left and right. With each step, we move too far off in one direction and we have to balance by coming back to the other direction.

Sometimes we lose our balance entirely. What our bodies are telling us at that moment when there's discomfort or stress is that there's a state of evolution that's occuring — physical evolution. Something new is being programmed into the biological system. Perhaps it won't manifest itself for another seven hundred years, but something is being transformed.

We are a tiny little model of the bigger picture. Maybe I've been working to get something done and it's not getting done, so I'm frustrated. I want to yell; maybe I do yell, and I feel guilty. When that is going on in my microcosm, in the macrocosm — maybe five or six solar systems away — I've created a definite shift in consciousness.

We humans are made up of all of the

eternities, so when something's going on out there, it is reflecting back here. The discomfort we're feeling here is reflecting what's going on out there.

This is a very Indian (Native American) idea. Whenever we're dancing or having a ceremony, we know we're not just doing it for us. We're doing it for the the larger being, of which we are a microcosm.

I am totally convinced that what we're doing here is exactly what we came here to do. We just keep doing it and we know that we're effecting some other dimensions because of our work here. This happens because we have these physical bodies which are not really just flesh and blood and bone, but are actually Principal Ideas. We were created so that we could function here, so that we could play a role in the unfolding of all the multiple dimensions of wisdom and truth. This unfolding is happening because of what our physical anatomy is doing.

We were given a mind to think as part of an inducement for being here.

One of the things I've found out about human beings is that nothing can harm us. Certainly someone can kill us and they can torture us, but they can't really rub us out because we're set on this vibration that goes on and on forever and we just keep showing up in different places. We are consciousness.

symbols   In order to understand ceremony, we have to understand that symbols are themselves vibrations. When we see a line that is going up and down or is going horizontally in a letter of the alphabet, we have to know that those horizontal and vertical lines have power in and of themselves. We use symbolic letters, or symbolic forms like numbers, because they have mystical power. Numbers have resonating vibrations. The cosmos is made of three things: numbers, letters, and words or sounds. We are made up of numbers, letters, sounds.

The cosmos is created by symbols. When you combine planting and seeing, those together become a sound vibration — a symbol.

In the vastness of *ooh*, in that innocence, there are some qualities. One of those is *naa-peh-cho*, which means numbers.

Na is to manifest. *Naa-peh-cho* gives us focus, direction, lineage, a target. That is what the head is created from. In the physical anatomy of the human body, the head is numberness. Numbers are the reason that we appear with a head, or that anything appears with a head. The head is the first. It guides. The head of a movement is the one who guides the movement.

Naa-peh-cho:

Na brings into existence, and *peh* is preciseness. It is like the arrowhead or the head of a movement; it is leadership. It is very important that we have that precision or clarity, that we master and understand that focus.

Cho means everywhere — and then some! *Cho* is childlike innocence, connecting us to all other planes.

Again, *na* is to bring manifestation into existence. *Peh* means direction, focus. *Cho* means beauty that connects us to all of the heavenly things.

Numbers came into existence to open the corridor to high potential.

The letters on the other hand have to do with *cah-naa*, which means how the Self is designing itself on the surface of being. Letters are imprinting what *naa-peh-cho* is trying to say; letters are imprinting what that movement is designating.

And sound is *pa*, and that means the status quo. It means how the heart sees itself in relationship to the original circle of light. How the divine heart, the divine centeredness, or loving kindness is in relationship to the original design.

So now, with numbers, letters and sounds together, you have the head of a family, the head of a focus, that has imprinted itself within this medicine wheel, so that it knows what it is.

As we learn more of our relationship with our heart and our intent, which is the focus of numerology, and our sense of knowing, because it is imprinted with our psyche, we can get out of this wheel. The only thing that gets us out is personal enlightenment, and then universal enlightenment. At that point, however, as soon as we kick out of this wheel, guess what? We just go next door! We get into another circle. There are millions and millions of these circles.

chanting   All ceremony is to help us connect the world of purity, placement, awareness, innocence, and carrying the personal self to the next levels, which are the psychic, spiritual levels.

Chanting is one of the ways to do this. Chanting puts one's attention back into the very present. If you really concentrate on chanting, you are not thinking about what you are going to do tomorrow, or what you will do next week, or what you did last year. You are the actual chanting itself. Eventually, you can transcend the five vowel vibrations and go into an altered state or parallel reality.

I believe that you can do it if you do some other things, such as fasting with no food and no water. You can do it more easily with a group than as an individual. The group vibration is all around you and it is impinging upon your physical body. Your body is like a vibratory instrument. It is vibrating, and group chanting enhances this. Group chanting magnifies the effect because the whole body is feeling the vibration of many voices impinging upon it. The whole psyche then reverts to beauty that is completing new moments of clarity. We are singing clarity into rightful living.

I believe that the different ceremonies that

have been done through the centuries were done because they were trying to find the space which I call the realm of magic — white magic — where you create in a positive way the environment that will enhance the continuation of life in the physical body. For instance, if you are chanting and someone is being healed, that singing enables the person to get well, because at some point the body of the person who is being healed merges with the parallel reality so that when the doctor reaches in to heal something, it can be healed. It is healed in the parallel reality; it has been changed because those two worlds have merged. Through ceremony, we bring the two worlds into coexistence. That is where we can access the future, which exists in the parallel reality.

Normal reality is based on separation, which produces fear. The parallel reality is based on love. When we bring the two together, love can transform fear into healing potential.

A holy person can do this at will. Now what we want is for everybody to be able to do this when they choose to do it.

The culture of the United States is where it is because it is seeking a way by which to continue enhancing states of union. This is a way to carry the culture in order to enhance the beauty. The original idea was good, but it doesn't always end up that way. The direction twists. That is the reason we have technology moving too fast now, creating things faster than we can use them or digest them.

Technology is moving so fast because a couple of hundred years ago, we cut too many trees. Now how would cutting too many trees affect technology? The metaphor or the vibration of greatness is connected to trees. When we cut the trees, they fall to the earth. Like the feminine energy that falls from the noosphere into the biosphere where it manifests new material forms, the trees go from the vertical to the horizontal plane. This causes a different energy in the biosphere, creating more things at a faster rate. The trees have the sky energy, and when the sky energy falls, it jumps back up and it falls back down. It awakens the receptivity and creates the activity. As the trees hit the earth and bounce, the culture becomes more active. We create more technology, the population booms, wars erupt. All those things come from frenetic energy, caused by the cutting down of trees.

Indian thinking says: when you do something, be careful; because what you do is going to have side effects. It is not just cutting down trees, it is changing the whole energetic configuration of the culture. That's why we do the ceremonies. They can contribute to the shifts in consciousness for a culture within a geography. When we do ceremonies, we are working on the energies.

The true visionary knows that the original idea of any ceremony came from a vision. The vision told the person who received it everything that needed to be done in the ceremony. So there was absolutely no guesswork. When I get a vision, I am told exactly, step by step, how to do it, and if I don't do it right, then there are angels, or beings, that come from the other side and tell me that I made a mistake.

Once you agree to be a visionary, the above beings give you a vision, and you have to do it. You can't say no. Once we have decided to come to this earth, we have to live up to certain criteria, because what we are doing has a direct connection to what is going on in the other dimension. Each of us came here as a result of a vision. The planet had a vision, and as a result of that, you happened and I happened. Once the planet had a vision, then we came as a result of divine calling, divine longing. So we agreed to come down, and by the time we were born we had already been given a place on the planet. We were born to fulfill that vision. All the trials and tribulations are tests. Their purpose is to make us the best possible conduits to move energy through that world, to enhance creation. We come here to manifest. We come to live in the world of illusion, to be in states of awe.

It is possible for ceremonies to become empty of their power. If you continue to follow the original prescription, the process of a ceremony, the same form over and over, it will empty the ceremony. Yet there is a good reason for purists. They know that you have to do the ceremony right if you are in this ordinary reality. Now once you get out of ordinary reality, the form doesn't matter. Once you are connected to the parallel reality in which you have the potential of all of these vibrations, purity is no longer an issue for you. Nor is placement, awareness, carrying or innocence. You only have to deal with them insofar as where you happen to be at the time. Am I pure enough, or clear enough to move into this reality?

So I think that we first have to learn the concrete sense of carrying, placement, and innocence before we can appreciate the reality where we will no longer need them. Ceremony is to help us, by using these forms, and as we work through them, they put us in the place where the forms no longer matter. We go from concreteness into abstractness and from abstractness back into concreteness — from parallel reality to normal reality — until they finally merge.

We are trying to live in the present tense, totally here but totally in a space of paradise where the two are simultaneously occurring. That is achieved only when we work at it by continually purifying ourselves. Ceremony is the way to do this. It gives us these powers. Ceremony works because it is crying for a vision. By crying for a vision, I mean that the soul is longing for light, so it can drink it and thus fulfill its nature. If light — vision — is lacking, there is sadness.

There are a lot of sad people in our world. People may have an abundance of material things, but they still lack deep inner satisfaction. We can get fulfillment when we go to church for communion, or into the sweat lodge, or to a ceremony of some type. The ceremony fulfills the loneliness, fulfills the longing, and allows universal intelligence to come in.

the sweat lodge   Native people almost always do sweat lodges before other ceremonies, as a purification and a preparation. This is because we need to program our minds, we have to program our bodies so that when we go into the ceremony we can maximize what we're going to get out of it.

To do the ceremony, a sweat lodge is framed out with willow poles lashed together to create a domed, circular enclosure. The willows are covered with tarps, making it completely dark inside the lodge. Lava rocks are heated red-hot in a bonfire outside the lodge. In the ceremony, people crawl into the lodge and sit in a circle around a pit in earth at the center of the hut. Then a helper uses a pitchfork to lift the heated rocks one by one from the fire and drop them in the pit inside the lodge. The tarp is pulled over the doorway. Then water is poured on the rocks and hot steam fills the lodge. Sage and other sweet-smelling herbs are also sprinkled on the burning rocks, filling the lodge with beautiful aromas. Prayers are given honoring the four directions, one in each of four rounds. Between rounds the tarp is raised, cooling the air inside the sweat lodge. More hot rocks are taken from the fire and placed in the sweat lodge pit and then the doorflap is closed again. With the door closed, the inside of the sweat lodge is completely dark and gets very hot, so that people are soon covered with sweat. The sweating itself is a purification on a physical level, but even more powerful things happen on the psychic and spiritual levels.

When I'm going to build the sweat lodge, the first thing that I do is I dig the center of the sweat lodge where the rocks are going to go when we bring them in from the fire and put them in the center of the lodge. What I do is take the earth from that hole in the middle of the sweat lodge and I put it on the right hand side of the doorway (as you're facing in) to make a shrine where people can put things. That pile of dirt that has come from the center of the sweat lodge is heart energy. The shrine is made out of the heart, so whatever we put on the shrine gets blessed. On the shrine people might put their eyeglasses in order to receive better vision, or they might put, symbolically, a relative that needs healing. Or they might put a medicine bag there or they might put a peace pipe there — anything they want blessed.

Then when I'm building the sweat lodge I decide which directions are the east, south, west and the north, and I place the upright willows about a foot and a half apart in each of those four directions, so that the lodge will be oriented in the directions. The door of the lodge is on the west. Fourteen feet west of the door of the lodge, I dig a pit for the fire. The dirt taken from the pit I line out in a semicircle on the west side of the fire pit so it is like a reflector. This mound reflects firelight back toward the sweat lodge.

The fire and the fire pit is the masculine. The sweat lodge is the feminine. Once I have the upright willows that are going north, south, east and west, then I start making a circle around the uprights by tying willows on horizontally. The first circle might be about a foot off the ground, then I go up another couple of feet and tie another circle of willows, until I have the built frame of the sweat lodge.

I lay wood for the fire in the fire pit. I put four logs side-by-side in a north-south orientation and then five logs on top of those, side-by-side in an east-west orientation. The wood going north and south represents the four directions. The wood above that, going east and west, is for five other beings: one for the above direction, one for the below direction, one for the person who is preparing the sweat lodge (the self), one for the circle, and one for the fire. Then I put the rocks on top of that.

I like to use cedar for this fire, because when cedar burns it doesn't leave any ashes. If I have both cedar and a type of wood that leaves ashes, like piñon, I like to put the wood that leaves ashes on the bottom. Then I put the wood that doesn't leave ashes to cover the top of the rocks. That way the rocks get cherry-red hot, which is what I want. Otherwise, they get hot, but not *really* hot, and we get a lot of steam in the lodge, more than we do heat. The steam could burn the skin, and usually that's not what I want. What I want is a quality heat that isn't scalding water on the skin.

Sometimes, however, I want this real steam. When a person sweats with scalding steam, there are certain levels he or she will connect with psychologically that we don't connect with when we use the drier heat. We're probably in a better place to slip from consciousness as we know it to a higher consciousness. This is because we're so uncomfortable, the heat is so unbearable, that we think we are going to die physically. Then, when we don't die and we know we aren't going to die and we're just going to have to be there, the mind makes a quantum shift. Some people say we have died and we've come back, having reached another state of enlightenment. That happens very rarely — usually to new people, who aren't acclimated to the sweat lodge.

Before I build a fire in the fire pit, I put in the rocks. I get rocks that are smaller than football size. Usually I use about eighteen sweat lodge rocks for a sweat. I start by putting a rock to the east side of the fire pit, then one to the south and one to west side of the pit and one to the north. Then I put one on to represent the above direction, one to represent the below direction.

Then I fill in the half-directions and the rest of the circle and stack them on top of each other.

Another thing I do is make a line of corn meal from the fire pit to the pit in the sweat lodge. I connect the fire pit to the heart of the sweat lodge in order to make a trail for the stone people to come along that path where the corn meal is into the other pit inside the lodge. Corn meal is the symbol of awareness.

What is going on in the sweat lodge? The heat is a metaphor for ancientness. When we feel the intensity of the heat, it affects our bodies, heating our skin. As soon as the heat hits our skin, we get lifted. This response is in the genetic code. Our bodies know we can go to a higher vibration; we can transcend everyday reality and reach the parallel reality. So we overheat the body. At some point, the heat will have to come down. The body will try to cool itself. At that break point, at the space in between heating and cooling, illumination enters. There is a burst of energy, like a drop of water in a hot frying pan, and in that instant the light comes.

The salt we have in our bodies affects this process. Sweating a little—maybe for five minutes—gets the salt and sugar out, so we can achieve that state.

The top of the sweat lodge is a metaphor for the galaxies, and so that is where the sacraments come together. It is a focal point. The rocks symbolize the earth and the first matter within the earth, the lava. Water, which is a metaphor for light, becomes steam as it strikes the hot rocks, and the steam in that context is the power of the rock emerging. This is the power of the Earth Mother and the Sky Father coming together. Steam is releasing the energy of the stone.

In the interaction between coldness and heat we have the process of evolution. We have movement and time. Ancient wisdom is the summer, movement is the winter. When we put movement with ancient wisdom we have a manifestation of matter, or some orientational formulation of mental, emotional, physical, or spiritual energies.

breath and chanting

We want to go beyond the ordinary through chanting, through singing. We get stuck in materialization; we are too materialistic, so that most of the unhappiness on the planet is the result of the soul not receiving its nourishment. When you go into ceremony through chanting, you bring time and future or past orientation into *cha,* which means *now*, and which also means *song.* In order to feed the soul, you have to come into the here and now. In truth, the here and now does not exist, only Divine Love that looks and feels like the here and now.

I read a book which studied black and white cultures and divided cultural attitudes into present-oriented and future-oriented. The present-oriented live just to survive; at least that was the premise of the study. I bring that up because Indians are present-oriented. The languages they speak are present-oriented, not because they want to remain nonproductive, but because to remain present-oriented is to access these alternate realities that we are talking about. This present orientation keeps you moving, and keeps you alive and connected.

Singing or chanting does something very special with time as it places the seeds of our aspirations into the framework of a future time and place. Most ceremonies in cultures all over the world use singing or chanting. This is because chanting in ceremony creates a pathway for beauty and awareness to merge into one essence.

As we start chanting, beauty, which has the physical properties of movement and cold, begins to heat up. Heat, which is ancientness, begins to flow into the cold of beauty, and as soon as this happens, the ceremony begins to move the cold truth from the ground level upward, toward a higher purity. This movement can be explained as heat pushing coldness from the floor level upward to the ceiling. Hot air penetrates the cold air as it rises. In the same way, the truth penetrates our consciousness as it rises, taking us to higher points of illumination.

As the truth rises and purifies, our intention in doing the ceremony is being carried into the future where it will be realized. For example, let us say that we are doing the ceremony in March for better crops in the summer. As we chant, that beauty rises, merges awareness with heat, and we become aware of a new illumination which can now be realized in the material realm.

Chanting affects our bodies on a cellular level, and it affects all the earth and plants as well. It clears away blocks so that life energy can flow uninterrupted; it frees stuck energy in the physical world around us.

Chanting also brings new energy from the heavens, from the noosphere, into the biosphere.

Everything in the biosphere is the result of principal ideas which lie latent in the noosphere and come to earth for materialization. Chanting connects us with those principal ideas and helps bring them into form.

Plants do not just grow up from the ground searching for sunlight. The sky, or noosphere, is pulling the plants up into itself. These principal ideas take material form as plants in order to embody something that has been latent in the noosphere all along. Chanting helps this process by unblocking their life energies and connecting them to the new energies from the noosphere. We are the environment creating more environments for us to live into.

In Tiwa belief, there is a direct connection between our conscious illuminations or thoughts and what our future experiences will be. By making a conscious connection with the new energies and principal ideas which are latent in the noosphere, we form a bridge between the heavens and the earth, and between the present and the future. In the singing part of the ceremony, the chanting creates a premonition of some future time by creating the future in the here-and-now time frame. In chanting, we plant the here-and-now with the seeds of our intentions for the future.

Hot is "oldness" that is filled with awareness, and purifies by burning the veil between the ancient wisdom and the here-and-now. In a sweat lodge, the intense heat heats up our bodies. This brings a shift in consciousness. Heat puts us in touch with ancient wisdom. When the heat of ancient wisdom encounters cold awareness, there is movement, merging, and this creates a premonition which is to be acted upon. We now have the ability to see into all of the eternities that create potential possibility.

The ceremony awakens through focus and movement the productive force of nature and implants by programming into the future a given, expected result. Actually, both the future and the past are here in the present, but they are in a parallel reality. Ceremony brings the ancient past into the present so we can learn from it. And ceremony also brings the future into the here-and-now and imprints it. Within intent is the energy to imprint the future. As soon as the chant or ceremony is over, the future goes back to the parallel reality and waits for us to show up five or six months later.

The planet eats the effort we expend, our prayers, sacred chanting, group worship, or our exertion in physical work. This is what the planet lives on.

Just as the heat of the sun on the surface of the earth creates humidity which rises to form rain clouds, the heat of our prayers, chants, or physical effort rises into the noosphere, where our thoughts and ideas ferment into our next earthly experience. These ideas become actions to be taken by us humans.

All our new discoveries and inventions start at this level before they descend into our conscious minds. It is the effort that we place on our daily attempts to reach our highest physical, mental, emotional, and spiritual potential that the planet uses to survive.

It is the role of the adult to try to keep the firm stability of the status quo going on so that the children can have available to them the solid foundation to build upon. It is the role of children as they become old enough to contribute to the planet to apply a certain amount of effort to make their ideas known. This effort the children put out in order to succeed is what the planet eats.

The earth, in its survival mode, will enhance any new ideas the child might seek to implement on the planetary scene. This is because the earth plans with us every new thing we do here. Whatever we do today will affect the seventh generation down the line.

When you do a vision quest, it is a way to feed the soul. You merge back into the soul—this idea of *chai ka*. *Chai ka* means to plant a seed, and the seed creates life. *Ka* also means to dream. (*Ka* also means buffalo, and buffalo is a metaphor for the four pillars of truth that are dreaming states that make up the reflective universe we know as perceptual reality, which is illusionary.)

In this dream of material reality, we eat to stay alive, and other things are eating us to stay alive.

Life, death, rebirth, all are part of this paradigm, this realm, this dream. In the ceremony, at some point, we go beyond this realm. It is no longer applicable.

light For me, the soul in metaphor is the process of drinking light. Light is universal intelligence and love, and it can't be stuck in the dark. What happens when the soul does not eat? It begins to dry up. Loneliness and separation are the results of the soul's lacking nurturing. So it is a continuous process to connect a soul to this flow of light or love. When it is fed, out of that comes genuine fulfillment. It just knows it is loved and cared for, and all that it must then do is stay in touch with light-filled creativity. It wants to create perceptions that are full of light.

I think in some ways that this is what the sound chambers are about. In 1984, I received the vision to build peace chambers or sound chambers — circular chambers where people chant together to bring about peace. Now forty-two such chambers have been built all around the world. They come now at this time to remind us, even if we never chant in them at all, that there is a concrete form where there is more going on here and now in the physical plane to connect us to the spiritual plane than we can ever understand.

About three months after I got the original idea of the peace chamber, I had another vision. I was taken out of my body and brought before a ring of elders, and they asked: "Why haven't you started building those peace chambers?" I said that it was because I couldn't find a place to build them. Next thing I knew there was a ring that came down from the heavens, showing me to build the first one next to my own trailer house in Bernalillo. And then a second ring came down, and there was an angel holding a little child. The angel placed the child on the earth in the center of the circle of light. Then I heard the angel's voice say: "This child is for you to raise." I was supposed to be the foster father for it. It was like an idea that had come down.

Up and down are a metaphor for receiving something and giving back oneself. That's what is going on with ascending and descending light: giving and receiving at the same time. So what we have here is a new child given to the earth. The earth is a symbol of the inifinite Self, the vast Self; that is what the soil is. And the grass is ancientness.

So, the child was given to the earth. A few months later I was doing some lectures in Marin County, California. There was an educational institute, right on the cliffs, for the Sufis order, and I did a sweat lodge there. At some point I was pulled out of my body and was taken underneath the ocean. There were three men who appeared and then I went down to the ocean floor. I remember falling off the cliff. They jumped off the cliff and their force drove me out of my body, and pulled me and I could see them. All three dove into the water and there were three white splashes—and I was falling; I was nothing but light.

Next thing I was in the corridor, like an underground tunnel, and the last one of them was in front of me and was pulling me along. He was like a man with shoulder-length blond hair, but also like a fish, a green fish. A merman. I saw him come into the light, and then, when I looked, I was in a big cabin all of a sudden, and there was no water.

There was this beautiful being sitting on a glowing throne studded with emeralds and diamonds. He had a cape that was blue, and an almost childlike face, a baby's face. There was a pink color, very pleasant, very calm, very beautiful, and he put a light in front of him that looked like a blue tear drop.

He communicated with me telepathically. He said, "I want you to go back, and on the seventh of April I want you to build a fire in the chamber. It is for the purification of the oceans." I knew that he meant physical oceans, and that he also meant the cosmic ocean. And he said the light of the fire needed to be reflected against the wall.

So then I went back and did the fire ceremony. In a flash of light I had been given all the details for the ceremony. In the vision, the steps were included, and it turned out that the logs for the fire were to be laid out like a tic-tac-toe grid.

So I started doing fire ceremonies every month on the seventh. As peace chambers were built, I instructed the people to do these fire ceremonies every month on the seventh. I instructed them to do that so when April came around they wouldn't forget. Later I found out in the literature that the Greeks used to honor Oceanus on April 7 by making a fire. Maybe the being in the ocean was Oceanus or a manifestation of him.

Oceanus is the metaphor for the birth of new ideas — babies. When we talk about the birth of babies, we are not just talking about the physical two-legged ones. We are talking about childhood in any dimension, as an idiom, an energy. Oceanus came to plant something new on the planet. I took his ceremony and I built a fire, and with that fire he was there.

Fire is the seed in the womb-like peace chambers. Birth is reflected off the walls from the center of the room.

There is a child that has been conceived in this womb space, and nurtured over the years. Now it is fourteen years old. I have known that the child would start teaching when it was about fourteen.

So I've been given this child, this fire. When the fire is kindled during the fire ceremony in the peace chamber, the light hits the wall, and it comes back and there is a rebirth in there. Maybe the light that comes out of the walls energizes the planet on some level metaphysically. It is bouncing off the walls of cosmic consciousness. Consciousness expands as the light touches it. There is now more that is knowable.

I have been taking care of my child given to me in vision for fourteen years, and I still don't know the full meaning of my vision. I keep caretaking, because that is my responsibility.

Indian religion has to do with developing the visionary capacities of the whole world tribe and of the individual people in it. We acquire these visionary capacities through dance, singing, chanting, and ceremonies, and by keeping that visionary status in the community and following the advice of the tribal visionary.

We're not doing this over here in the concrete world. In the concrete world, experience seems to be the important thing. Get it done!

But the visionary would get visions for the tribe to enhance the life of the tribe as a whole. The various ceremonies or dances tribes have are based on actual visions that people had. We no longer remember what the purpose was in the beginning, but now it's a buffalo dance, a deer dance, a sun dance, an eagle dance. In time, the people who had the visions died, but the other people kept these ceremonies going.

aroma   When a holy person or a visionary teacher dies, he comes back and teaches his students in their dreams and enters their intuitive knowing. I think my grandfather stayed around for a while. Twenty years after his death, I received an illumination that carried his imprint; I could smell him. He had a smell like rose petals. I could identify him with that smell by the time I was five or six years old. Many years after he died, I was still getting teachings from him—insights—and when they would come I could smell my grandfather's scent of rose petals.

That's also how I remember my foster mother. She really loved red roses, and she and my foster father had yellow roses. They grew them in two different areas up on the ranch. The roses weren't anything elaborate, there were just one or two plants, but my foster parents really loved them. I remember that I gave her sixteen red roses when she had been very sick. I had just gotten out of graduate school, and I walked into her room with roses. I remember the smile on her face when I gave her the roses.

The next day, she died. When I entered the house, I heard this voice say: "don't look to the right, but just go straight into the bathroom." As I went in, I smelled a very strong scent of roses.

Scents and aromas manifest by the purity of innocence that is connecting itself to the energy of relationships. They manifest by the power of loving connections. I pray for all my relations when we are praying in the sweat lodge. I want love. I want good rain. I want abundance for all my relations. Aroma was created out of these particular powers, when they merged together. It was the merging of these resonating vibrations that put together the essence or meaning of aroma. The reason aroma therapy works is that it carries the power of purity and innocence made of loving kindness.

What is that power, the purity of innocence? It has to be lovely, because it is so sincere. Innocence doesn't want anything. It doesn't demand anything. It doesn't care whether it succeeds or not. It is just pure, and this aroma is pure innocence that has fused to the capacity to manifest connections, so that all things that exist may be blessed. The connection makes us true brothers and sisters. It is like love. Innocence connects itself to everything that is.

Aroma is a way of connecting to that aspect of everything which is childlike innocence. Aroma is another way to hear something through smell, or see something through smell. It is a calling; we follow a scent. That is why incense is used in ceremony. Everything in life is a metaphor for an idea, and an idea is God's presence in our lives.

Sage, for instance, creates the energy that is necessary for us to transcend and to go into the depths of the inner self. Cedar doesn't do that; cedar has to do more with the journey that we are on, the journey in this world, whereas the sage has more to do with inner work. So when we inhale the aroma, it connects us to these qualities.

cooking and imprinting   Ceremony
connects us to the principal ideas. What are
principal ideas? For instance, let's say perceptual
reality is a principal idea. In the beginning of time,
before the process of cooking food was created,
we didn't have perceptual reality, because
perceptual reality and cooking are the same. We
couldn't perceive anything until we learned to
cook, or maybe perception is what created
cooking. The process of materialization is when an
idea gets "cooked" into a perceivable reality.

Everything is connected to something. I think
the idea behind perceptual reality and cooking is
imprinting. That is what the eyes do. They see
something and they say, "It's mine, it belongs to
me," and there's a heat that is sent out. The heat
goes out, hits the form, changes it in some way and
returns it to the perceiver so that now it belongs
to perception.

How many principal ideas are there? There
could be as many as seven or fewer. There isn't a
list. Everything in this reality is but a reflection of
something that is out there somewhere, that is a
principal idea. There is falling, running, walking,
dreaming, standing, lying down, growing; these can
all be connected to principal ideas.

Somewhere something is holding the energy
of growingness so that everything is growing here.
Little children are growing, plants are growing,
trees are growing, and the only time they don't
grow is when there is too much *chi*, so that they

go into the dreams, go into the cold.

We should try to live our present lives as well as possible, because how we live now, how we treat people, and how we treat ourselves is what we will get in the future. Because it is imprinting. We are putting something there that later on we are going to eat. We are cooking our future.

Because we live in the form world in which everything around us is form, after a while we tend to think in terms of form. But actually, we are not forms, we are energies that are creating the forms. Then we begin to believe in the form, and we become the form. I can say I am a carpenter, or I'm a janitor, or I'm a housewife, or a publisher. Pretty soon, we take on the attributes of the role, but actually, we are formless. In order to find our place, our true place, we teach ourselves to go back to knowing that everything around us is a form, but it is a form that we have created on some level. It is us but in a different form—a different expression of us.

Gold, for instance, is the symbol of the beauty of the light, of the universe of intelligence. Myrrh is the vibration of how manifestation is carrying its resonance. Frankincense has to do with the way we initiate our faith to beauty. It was appropriate that gifts of gold, frankincense, and myrrh be given to Jesus, because that's what Jesus was. Gold is beauty in action. I can understand why the alchemists were trying to turn things into gold, because gold is a metaphor for purifying the self.

Beauty is like divine purpose that has a loving resonance with the All-that-is. Beauty is the focus for the resonance with All-that-is. It is carrying crystallized awareness.

I've spent all my life trying to explain actions with metaphors so that in time, if I can keep going and practicing and thinking this way, eventually the metaphor and the thing are going to merge and become one.

Water is used in many ceremonies because it has to do with light. The essence of water is blessing someone with light. For instance, when water is used in baptism, it connects all of the heavens with innocence; innocence and the heavens become one. And you can't improve on that concept! Water is all the heavenly planes coming in simultaneously at every level. It is all going on simultaneously with one drop of water on your forehead. When you get baptized, it is innocence and all the heavens, captured in water that is light.

When blood first began to flow in the anatomy of beingness it was saying "yes" to light. Beingness could now manifest in all its different multiplicities in blood. The hunter who killed an animal would drink the blood of the animal, because in drinking the blood he became the vibration of the principal idea of that animal. It is a communion with the soul of the animal. Then the deer is you, the lion is you. At some level, originally, when people ate meat, they didn't eat because they were hungry, or because they wanted to become carnivorous. They ate the meat because that's how they could connect with a principal idea or vibration, an archetype, as they were divinely guided.

Scientists tell us we have a reptilian brain and a mammalian brain within our human brain. Whenever these ancients ate food from these different forms — the birds, reptiles — it was because we have aspects in common. When they ate the meat, they were eating themselves. They were connecting with those parts of themselves. Whenever we eat a plant, in the process of digesting that plant, we receive certain forms of illumination. So I think the diet has to do with purpose. Because the ancient ones ate animals, we don't have to.

If you want to be a visionary, you should eat the meat of a lion, either actually or symbolically. If you want to be a person who has a direct line, to be able to correctly define the metaphors that depict wisdom, you might want to drink deer blood.

We take into our bodies the things that feed the soul. We take in a vibration. Unless we eat knowing that we are taking in a vibration, we get stuck in the form, without realizing that we are not form. While we can recognize a form and give it a place, we need also to honor the idea that we are non-form, because beyond the form is another form, a more eternal, spiritual form.

I think of the Christian communion in which Christians symbolically drink the blood and eat the body of Christ. Bread comes from the wheat, a plant. When you are eating the body of Christ, you are taking on "Christ-like" qualities. The bread is the closest thing we can find to connect with the reasons that the Self is being and doing what we are being and doing at this time. It is a way to get in touch with the path, or rather, to become the path itself — the path that is resonating right out of the inifinte self. That is what "breadness" means. Bread is the light of beauty, which is what Christ was. When we eat the bread of Mother Earth in holy ceremony, we are giving respect. The main thing that ceremony teaches is respect. It teaches respect for oneself, for tradition, for other people, other people's traditions, other people's ways, for the enhancement of life.

judgment   If someone is doing something that I don't think is right, the first thing I question is what role are they playing at this time on the planet. What is their real role, and is this what they are supposed to be doing? I ask those questions, rather than going on into judgment, because when I go into judgment, I know I am calling judgment onto myself. Judgment tends to block the divine process of life, not only for yourself, but for others. So you don't want to judge too much because you end up with other people judging you. You create more of that kind of energy. Then you pick up judgment because that thought you put out is still around you. You create a hindrance for your own process through judgment.

Ceremony teaches us that everything that comes around goes around, and that what we create is empowered by us to go around the circle of life. Eventually it comes back. It may come back in two or three seconds or two or three weeks, but it eventually comes back. Everything that we give returns to us, and that is the whole idea of the reflective universe. That's metaphor alongside our experiences.

In the beginning, everything was unity, but now we are living in the time of diversity. For this reason, we need to be careful about what thoughts we have, because as soon as we have them they are going out, and eventually they are going to come back. If our thoughts are positive, we are going to get positive stuff back, and if our thoughts are negative, we get negative coming back.

So, rightful living is important, because we are creating now what we are going to live tomorrow. Ceremonies of the living spirit teach us respect for that line of thinking.

It is all right for people to be where they are because that is how far they have gotten from where they started. Sometimes they actually have achieved even more than we have because they are coming from a place farther along the line.

Except that it doesn't always look that way to us.

Someone who is alcoholic or homeless actually may be a hundred thousand years ahead on his karma for doing that. He is suffering the cold out there, probably with no food, and maybe his liver is going out because he drank too much. All this suffering may be moving him further along karmically than we are. Who are we to judge what is going on with him, except that if we judge him, then at some point we are creating an energy that will judge us. That judgment means that when you judge somebody and it comes back, it makes it more difficult for your process; that judgment gets in the way. It is not even someone judging you now, it is just an energy.

carrying and letting go   Through ceremony there is a way of not carrying fatigue or problems from day to day. Through ceremony you deal with the problems so they don't usurp your energy, and the next day you start new.

The key to this discipline, this ceremony, is in a Tiwa word. *Tsclo-ii-eh* means "one is at rest." It is the combination of three energies, descending light, childlike innocence, and awareness. That is what heals you from tiredness. So your ceremony should combine these three energies: descending light, childlike innocence, and awareness.

One of the physical manifestations for awareness is water, so you want to take a shower or a bath. As you are doing that, you just let go of today's worries. But it's not just a bath. For it to work as ceremony, the intention has to be there.

You could say the word *"tsclo-ii."*

Tsclo means rain that's falling on a parched landscape. When rain falls it gives new light. That is the metaphor. That's the descending light, but it's the feminine because it's birthing, it's ever-growing. It's nurturing, it's a nurturing waterfall, nurturing rain. You say, *"tah tsclo-ii-eh." "Tah"* is "I am," so *"tah tsclo-ii-eh"* means "I am the one that's in a state of nurturing — a state of awareness, a state of innocence, a state of descending light."

Doing this ceremony will free you of the problems of yesterday without causing you to lose the thread of what you were doing. Anything manifesting in your life is an energy so strong it won't let you forget it. But when it does come to you the following day you're in a different continuum, so it's in a different layer. It's not impinging on your life any more, and you deal with it from an impersonal plane.

This is the ceremony: get in the bath or shower and meditate on falling rain and on nurturance. Just let everything wash, because you're transforming yourself into a new being, into a new seed, into a new resonance. And then once you do it, don't second-guess it. Of course the mind will say, "Did I do it right? Did I do it long enough? Did I do it to the depths that I should?" Don't worry about anything. Just do it, and then go to bed. After doing it for three or four nights (or three or four weeks at the most), then the body just knows to do it.

Sometimes people will ask me about things we were discussing together three or four weeks before, and I don't remember what they are talking about. That's because, when I give a thing energy, at that moment I give it all the energy, all the focus, that needs to go into it. It's a new day. Tomorrow I may not feel about today's concerns the way I did today because tomorrow is another day. I gave it all the attention it needed today and so tomorrow I focus on something else.

Being able to let go is important when I am working as a healer. The way I do it is I listen to the Tiwa word *kaa who*. *Kaa* means to heal; *who* means the presence of God. *Kaa* means something that is buried within. That's what I am healing or stimulating to be healed. That person has something buried that needs to be healed.

Kaa who. The very word tells you that when you're going to work with someone as a healer you're working with the inner resources or the inner self. When you work as a healer, you also know that you're not doing the healing yourself. You are just half of the process. The other half is God. God is the one that's going to carry it through. Therefore, you don't end up holding or carrying the illness. If you end up getting sick, that means that you are not totally in alignment with the power that's coming from the Great Spirit. Early on, good healers realize that they are not the ones that are doing the healing, but they're assisting. When I work with people as a healer, I just let the healing energy go through me, and I don't hold on to it.

a "telephone dance"   We came out of ceremony. All of life came out of ceremony. When a person is sitting alone in a room, that is a ceremony. In groups or whole tribes, people connected to ceremony by doing bear dances or grass dances. I know this may sound foolish, but today an individual in a building might do a window dance, or a book dance, or a lamp dance, or a desk dance, or a telephone dance, or a bed dance. He can have a vision about that, or maybe I have the vision for people who can't have a vision right away.

Here is how you might have a vision for a "telephone dance":

How many vowels are there in telephone? You have the "eh" and the "oh" sounds, so you start making those sounds, those vibrations. You stop eating—no food, no water—and you sit in the room, and you start chanting that sound, repeating that sound, *eh-eh-oh*. Maybe you do it five hundred times, chanting it slowly, or you might do it quick in two minutes until you have a vision or you have an impulse of a ceremony to do. Then you do the ceremony. You don't do it

for any other reason than to move yourself
into the expanded reality where love and
fear bond and become infinite knowing.

Maybe your hands hold stones, and that
would be the ceremony for the filing cabinet.
And so you do that ceremony. You can
access the metaphor. Find the archetype—
"the great filing cabinet in the sky."

You go all the way back to the thing that holds
the memory. That is the pattern of everything.
Original ceremony is a living thing. It's alive in our
gene pool. Actually, we are doing ceremony
constantly, in spite of ourselves. When an office
worker walks up to the filing cabinet and pulls out
a drawer and reaches in and pulls out a file, and
then puts it back, that is a ceremony because the
office worker is moving forward, moving back.
When you are sitting down, that is a holy posture;
when you stand up that is a holy posture; when
you walk out the door that is a holy posture. The
door itself is a holy posture, a metaphor. I think
secretaries are blessed because they file and use
computers.

Can you imagine all kinds of people doing a
dance about a filing cabinet? Yet every object,
every form carries a principal idea. All these
forms that are around us are simply us, things that
look strangely different, images that come out of
the archetypes of the living spirit. Ceremony itself
is a living spirit. We talk about breaking our rigidly

controlled concepts, which don't actually exist, but we find that when we use ceremony, it opens the principal idea behind everything around us. That is what the Christian missionaries didn't understand when they came to us four hundred years ago. They said, "You are dancing to a tree! That is the silliest thing you can do. You are worshiping everything but God, because God wants a church." To them, dancing to a tree was pagan.

What the prehistoric peoples were trying to do was go through that doorway to get to the Source. We need ceremony to nurture us, but what we really need to know is how our lives are ceremonious. In that way, we understand that we are being nurtured. Yet, in order to understand, we still have to do the dance. One, two, three, four, five and then you back up to the wall, and swoop down twice. That's the dance for the filing cabinet which was originally a big pot with a scroll in it. That is the ceremony that you do for that. You are not really doing it for the filing cabinet, but for the principal idea.

When you walk up to the filing cabinet and open it, read something, put it back in and shut the drawer, that is also ceremony, but not a formal ceremony. Dance means expansion. The reason for doing the ceremony is to expand the principal idea. You can dance to expand anything. If you want to know more about what this pen is, you dance it to find out. What is the door in terms of metaphor? If you can create a door dance, then eventually you can find out why buildings have doors. I promise you that it is not to have an opening to a room, nor to shut out the outside or inside. Knowledge, wisdom, insight comes from the expansion.

You want to start with what you already have. Start with chanting. Chanting brings everything into the here and now. It opens like a door and you can see through. You have to sing to the telephone, to make the ceremony. Sing to the bowl. Sing to a deer that is lying there in ceremony because it has been shot by the hunter. Sing to all of the different parts. The horns, the skin, the inner organs are open, full of ideas.

The chant to the telephone would be "*eh, eh, oh. Eh, eh, oh.*" It is saying placement, placement, childlike innocence in which the self connects to other beings. Write the word *telephone*:

t - e - l - e - p - h - o - n - e

Study the word. What does the "t" suggest? The "t" tells us that one of the things that the telephone is doing for us here is trying to help us achieve an even higher potential than we are achieving now. When God created the phone for us — when one day through technology we would have a phone — one of the reasons it was created was that it would push us to want to achieve a higher purpose than before the telephone.

When I do the telephone dance one of the things I will look for is to try to see if at some point during the ceremony I am going to find a corridor in which I can go beyond what I am doing right now as a human being to something more. Higher potential becomes a motion. God is breath, matter, and movement.

Look at the next sound. The "eh" has to do with placement, so you put down placement. Now the *l* is a vertical line that makes a connection to all of the heavenly planes. What I see in this word is a grid, and the energy is coming into the grid down this vertical line. It shows that we have something pushing us toward our highest psychic potential.

Notice that the placement is followed by the letter *p,* which signifies heart. So the phone is trying to find us a heart. The letter *h* has to do with everywhereness. If consciousness were a whole bunch of dots, *h* connects us with all those little dots, all reality. *H* is universality. *O* has to do with innocence, playfulness, childlikeness. *N* is the self. Notice that it is connected with innocence of the self. If you look you see *one* there. *O-n-e.*

One of the things you want to teach your mind to do is to look at patterns. Look for patterns in the word telephone. You see *one,* then there is the *n* and the *e* again which is, again, placement.

So, having understood all those things, you review them for two or three minutes: placement, heart, universality, childlike innocence, self. Review those, but try not to think about them. Just repeat "eh-eh-oh-eh." (Does it matter that the final e is silent? Go ahead and pronounce it.)

You are repeating this word now, and at some point when you least expect it, an image appears in your consciousness. An image will come. The image may be the motion you are supposed to make, or maybe a cedar tree, a cedar branch appears, or a screwdriver. Then you chant this new word you've been given. You keep chanting. It is a process of elimination. The mind is very resistant, but then at some point your body will start to move. You get the dance. You have to forget your body consciously and you get to the point where you know the body is there, but you are not controlling it. At some point, you will intuitively know the step. But you have to trust it and in the beginning you won't. Keep at it until you break through and the body takes over. You are standing and then you chant, you close your eyes, you begin to sway, you allow your body to move in the chanting. You might begin stepping around, moving your arms. Then you practice it, write it down. Then the next time you want to dance to the telephone, including the spiritual realm, you do the same dance.

Let me go back to the world culture and the reason we have the telephone, or tape recorders, or desks, or lamps. We think we have them because it makes things easier for us, but I think if we really understood it from the place of metaphor, we would understand that these things are God talking to us. We can discover where we are spiritually in terms of the things that we use to make our daily living. They will help us discover our own imagery. They make up our life ritual.

Life was created, and all of the different physical forms, or mental forms, or emotional forms are created in our search for our beauty. Beauty is the only thing that is real. Everything else we do, we are doing in order to find beauty in ourselves.

One of the ways to find that beauty is through ceremony. We have gotten away from ceremony because we went too far toward the rational side. The rational mind says: "Oh, that's not real, not important, it's ridiculous." Or, "I don't need ceremony because I understand what is behind ceremony." But something very important happens when we dance that form. It brings the form into the body as beauty and awakens in the gene pool the knowledge of the principal idea that created the desk or the lamp. The body is part of our knowing. In the process of dancing (the motion or movement) we become the divine breath, creating new ideas for us to live by.

We need ceremony because our souls are dying of thirst. Remember, dancing is expansion. Expansion is moving us from the thing that is imprisoning us. We are breaking free.

Expansion increases our capacity for breath. Since we come out of breath, not out of movement, we have to go back to breath. Breath has to do with expansion.

So, we receive the ceremony and have definite instructions: we know the first step, the kind of singing, the kind of chanting, the duration, how often we're supposed to do the ceremony, the time of the year it should be done, or if it should be done in the morning or the afternoon. Then, once the ceremony is set, at some point we get an intuitive sense that we have to make a change in the ceremony that will make it slightly different than the original design that we got. That is the unexpected.

Now here is what is important about the unexpected: When we have been doing the dance in a particular way for the last three times, and all of a sudden we get this intuition that we need to do it differently, what's really happened is that there is a crack that opens from the infinite vastness in which a gift has come through our ceremony to the planet and to the whole cosmic consciousness. We get an unexpected insight; we will feel it as a jolt; it will shake us. Now that is the real stuff, coming directly from our Maker. It hits us. That is the unexpected. The reason it does that is because that is the only way it knows to impress us with some new input, to come and touch us. Most of us go through life asleep, thinking that we are awake.

Otherwise there are guides, or gatekeepers in the four directions, keeping information out so that everything can stay the same. They are mental, emotional, spiritual, physical gatekeepers. Energy is coming in and going out. Gatekeepers won't let anything new in unless we can slip it past the gate. Ceremony is one way to slip things past the gatekeepers. The unexpected is when we have a basic idea of how things are going to go for us that day, but on the way to the car, the unexpected happens, and we fall down.

Let's really study this momentarily. We slip and fall, and we weren't expecting to fall. At the moment when we begin to fall—and we wish we could do something about it, but we can't—that's the only point where we are truly in a place of total and complete detachment.

Maybe the cosmos was created because God was walking down the steps and he slipped and fell. When he slipped, this reality was created between the time he started to fall and when he hit the ground. We were made from an accident. We kind of slipped between the cracks.

When the unexpected happens, that's when something new can come in. That is what brings about evolution—the necessary unexpected. I believe this very deeply. In fact, I live my life always praying for the unexpected, because the unexpected always brings wonderful gifts that I never thought were possible or could happen. I guess I get set in my ways, about how I think things should be. The unexpected re-charges my energy as it gives me a whole new idea about the way things really are.

ceremony and the mind of God

Who is God?" the student asks.

And the Sufi answers, "Yes."

The Sufi has answered in metaphor, in a pun, because "*Hu*" means *God* in the language of the Sufi.

Puns, metaphors, parables, and stories are the teaching tools of the spiritual teacher in every tradition, including mine. Metaphors connect the world around us with the metaphysical, giving us a window on the infinite.

"Is metaphor not simply a figure of speech?" the student asks, and the answer comes:

"Metaphor is how God is present in our lives."

We think in godly ways because metaphor is energy that is in a state of action, breathing life into ceremony.

"What, then," the student asks, "is ceremony?" The answer to this question is that ceremony is how we, "the people" (vibration) are crying for a vision.

"What does it mean to cry for a vision?" the student asks.

And the teacher says: "Crying is how the souls of the people are drinking the sounds, 'aah, eh, ii, ohh, uu,' the vowel sounds that occur in all languages. At the same time God (Higher Power) is providing the living inspiration (breath) of life to that process."

God is in everything. As we work with metaphor, we discover the connections among all things; we enter the No-mind, God's mind. We become poets and artists, composers, seeing everything through the poetic, artistic, musical mind. We see things from metaphor and are filled with awe. At that moment we're coming from a base of love rather than a base of fear, because fear is an attribute of the rational, thinking mind. Through metaphor we can go beyond the rational, to enter the all-loving, all-pervading mind of God.

Our rational, thinking mind does not disappear. It is fused with the metaphoric mind, the mind of God. In the metaphoric mind, there is righteousness, based in love. The metaphoric mind swallows up the fear-based thinking mind.

Now, our souls no longer hunger for peace and solitude, because at every moment the soul is being fed from this place of love. No longer are we stuck on the surface of the material, but we have gone through the material to reach its essence. Our souls are drinking the light of the essence of the material plane. The loving mind of God has swallowed the thinking mind — owned it and swallowed it into the larger mind. At that moment all there is is love.

Everything that is perceivable to us is now

showing us how God is kissing all forms into life, through breath, matter, and movement. God gives sustenance to life.

In other words, metaphor is how God insists upon inspiring our innate, God-given gifts — gifts we received at birth — into fully awakened states so that we may materialize them throughout our living moments.

In order to become people full of awe for life, we enter, through metaphor, into ceremonies of the living spirit.

the stages of growth into consciousness

When we are born, we are born raw, and as we progress in life we get more "cooked" until eventually we are well done. We come unmarked and unformed, and we grow into perception through experience.

There are several levels of maturation that are required by Mother Nature for us to experience as we grow into women or men. They can be said to be stages of growth into consciousness. These are steps that women or men must go through, not simply because they are women or men. In each individual, the feminine or masculine needs to be born and nurtured so that that particular aspect of consciousness can grow.

The feminine is that aspect of life that is constantly in a state of flow. It is like descending light that can never stop without the masculine aspect. The masculine is that aspect of life that stops or tries to stop the flow in persons, places or things. The masculine is the aspect that falls from grace, because the flow is grace. Technology becomes possible with the masculine aspect.

When we learn, we work with three levels of energy: intellect, the intuitive, and the spiritual. The intellectual level involves the *maa* energy. We analyze, we take notes, we memorize. The intuitive level bypasses all this action of the intellect. It involves the *waa* energy. The spiritual involves *chi* energy, which is a higher vibration still.

Life is made out of a chain of events somehow similar to the unfolding of a normal day and night. Your day (or your life) might unfold somewhat like this example:

Step 1: You awake out of physical sleep

Step 2: You wash, shower, and get dressed

Step 3: You eat breakfast

Step 4: You prepare to go to the office

Step 5: You travel to work

Step 6: You're at work when a phone call comes and stops the flow of the morning's events. The call is disruptive. It is the masculine at work. You stop the flow in order to start a different movement.

Remember that there is really no "up-and-down" continuum, but that we create these metaphors here in order to give purity, placement, awareness, innocence, and carrying a structure. Only when these are ordered in a structure can we perceive that which cannot be seen. After all is said and done, we are simply being and vibration.

Here are the stages of life (developing feminine energy) and their Tiwa names:

1. *Oh-tie* – fetus in the womb

2. *Oh-see-aah-who* – baby in the act of birthing

3. *Oh-see-aah-ii* – the moment at which the child takes its first breath

4. *Oh-chi-ack-key-aah-oh-nay* – baby (0 to 5 years old)

5. *Oh-oh-peeh-yo-nay* – little girl (5 to 6 years old)
   Oh-cho-oh-nay – little boy (5 to 6 years old)

6. *Oh-peh-yo-nay* – girl (6 to 14 years old)
   Oh-cho-nay – boy (6 to 14 years old)

7. *Oh-peh-yo-quol-ley-nay* – girl 14 to 16 years old
   Oh-cho-co-queh-nay— boy 14 to 16 years old

8. *Quol-ley-nay* – girl 16 to 20 years old
   Co-queh-nay — boy 16 to 20 years old

9. *Quol-lee-hue-way-nay* – woman 20 to 25 years old
   Co-queh-sue-may-nay – man 20 to 25 years old

10. *Lee-hue-way-nay* – woman 25 to 55 years old
    Sue-may-nay — man 25 to 55 years old

11. *Key-ah-tah-meh-nay* – Elder (55 to 75 years old) (It is only after he or she reaches this stage that a person can officially become a storyteller.)

12. *Lee-hue-lah-oh-nay* – Old woman (75+ years old)

Sol-thay-own-nay – Old man (75+ years old)

step 1: Both the feminine and masculine are teaching the baby. *Oh-tie* is teaching during the different embryonic stages inside the womb. *Oh-tie* teaches the child to be open to learning as a forward and backward motion — to be open to learning by doing.

step 2: When the child is in the birthing process (vaginal canal), she is at the stage of *oh-see-aah-who*. *Oh-see-aah-who* teaches to be open to learning how placement purifies through polarity or struggle. Learning is infused into the psyche through struggle or polarity in order to move toward reconciliation, spiritual purpose, and transformational potential.

step 3: *Oh-see-aah-ii*, or the point where the child takes its first breath, is teaching the child how struggle or polarity invites awareness as self-identity. Before it takes its first breath, the child does not exist. Then the child breathes and it has an individual identity of breath, matter, and movement.

step 4: *Oh-chi-aah-key-aah-oh-nay* says that teachability comes through movement. Motion is the same as perceivable reality. Motion teaches while it purifies not only the personal self but connects all teaching to the vast Self as well.

Tu-caa, which means purifying, is the vibration which cleanses and sanctifies that which is learned. Now it can be seen as a body of beauty made of universal intelligence.

step 5:   *Oh-oh-peeh-yo-oh-nay*. At this stage the child is learning to reflect upon what it sees. On the feminine side, this reflection connects the spiritual body (that which inspires) with the heart body (that which feels). On the masculine side, the child is learning divine movement and how the psyche is always open to the learning which may be available internally or externally, from mental, emotional, physical, or spiritual bodies.

step 6:   *Oh-pee-yo-oh-nay* on the feminine side teaches how to connect seeing *(pee-yo)* with curiosity as receptivity. On the masculine side, meanwhile, the girl is learning to climb upward to find the beauty of new self-discovery. She climbs up in order to connect to the vast Self. In her individuality, that vast Self is grounded. In Tiwa thought, nothing exists unless it is grounded, unless it is based on the divine longing to exist.

step 7:   *Oh-peh-yo-quol-ley-nay* on the feminine side teaches the girl to bring separateness into her oneness, to become an individual. On the masculine side, she is learning that beauty and standing are the same, and standing means existing in oneness, as an individual.

step 8:   Here the girl or boy continues the lessons of *oh-peh-yo-quol-ley-nay* that were begun in the step above.

step 9:   This period of life teaches the person on the feminine side to continue to be receptive to new insights in order to keep renewing beauty. The masculine is teaching that beauty and standing existence must be substantiated by a spiritual life and death in order for renewal to occur. (Life is now seen not as a continuum so much as a series of deaths and rebirths through which the person's individual beauty is continually being renewed.)

step 10:   The feminine teaches the person that descending light comes bringing insight. The masculine teaches that divine longing is necessary for the person to move upward toward purity.

step 11:   The feminine teaches "mother-ness," or receptivity. The masculine teaches "father-ness," or activity. These two teachings combine as the Mother-Father-God principle. *Key-aah-ta-meh-nay* women and men are elders in the community. At this stage, they are considered well-done, well cooked, and can now teach the traditions because they have passed all the stages successfully and have acquired a deep understanding of "metaphor alongside experience."

step 12:   In old age, the feminine teaches that wisdom descends from above, while the masculine teaches that that which falls from above is full of ancient wisdom which can only be used or understood after it has been grounded on the physical plane.

Ian Robinson.
Palatine House
Preston